RKINA FASO

NEW LIFE FOR THE SAHEL?

(Jeremy Hartley/Oxfam)

A Report for Oxfam by Robin Sharp

CONTENTS

Designed by Oxfam Design/Mike Brain
Printed by Oxfam Print Unit

OXFAM

Published by Oxfam
274 Banbury Road
Oxford OX2 7DZ

ISBN 085598 130 X

ACKNOWLEDGEMENTS

Many people have given invaluable advice and practical help in the preparation of this book. In particular, the author wishes to express his gratitude to Mahamadou Kone, Yacouba Zeba, and all the staff of Oxfam in Burkina Faso for their encouragement and support. Thanks are also due to Jacques Giri, Chris Roche, Camilla Toulmin and Nigel Twose, whose comments on the manuscript provided important insights on a number of issues, as well as helping to avert some errors. Finally, special thanks to Sarata Sawadogo, Guiro Mahama, Demo Mamoudou, the Women's Group of Titao, and others too numerous to mention in towns and villages across Burkina who gave us their time, their thoughts, and their very generous hospitality. To them, their families and their future, this book is dedicated.

Approaching sandstorm near Titao, Yatenga province.
(Jeremy Hartley/Oxfam)

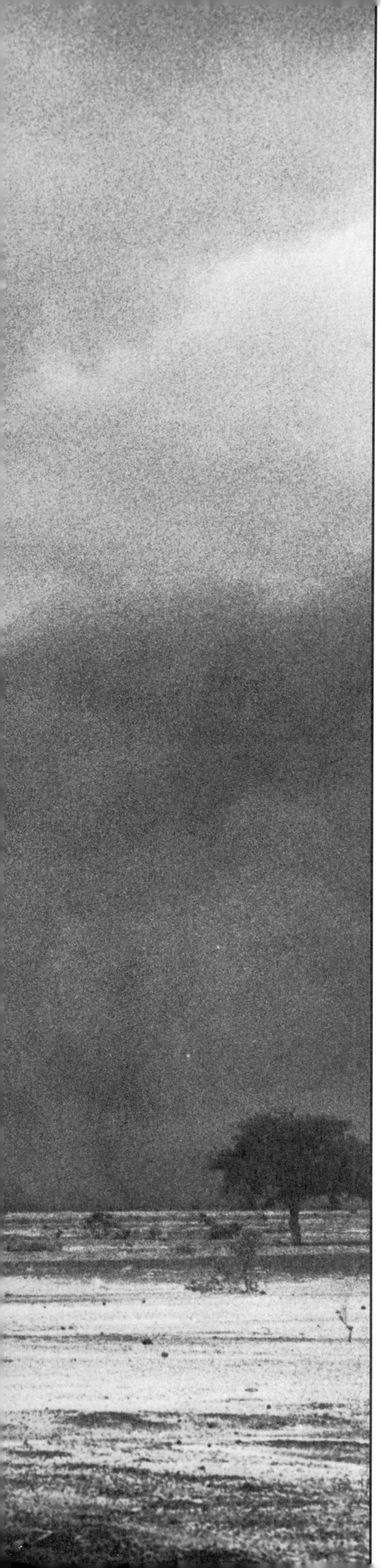

INTRODUCTION

This book is about a courageous but endangered people, and about their land, the land of their gods and their ancestors, a harsh land where the essential patterns and values of life withstood all challenges for a thousand years. It is about their collision with the twentieth century, their fortitude in the face of change all around them, and their dilemmas as they see their land now half-dying under the stresses of climate, cultural erosion, and misbegotten kindnesses.

Burkina Faso: 'Land of the People of Integrity'. A country of nine million people and 7,000 villages stretching from the arid fringe of the Sahara in the north to green landscapes in the south west. Many villages struggle against the odds for the barest survival; others are mobilising what resources they have, sometimes with a little outside help and encouragement, to try to regain control of their lives.

Revival in the Sahel? It is a tantalising question whether even survival — let alone revival — will be possible for this arid belt of land which forms the southern fringe of the whole Sahara desert and takes in Burkina's northern provinces. After twenty years of recurrent drought, the pressure of more people on fewer resources, and the uncertain impact of global warming still to come, the outlook, on the face of it, is scarcely promising.

Less than a quarter of Burkina's land area, in fact, qualifies as strictly Sahelian, receiving under 300 mm of rain a year, while the south and south west may get up to four times that amount. In between, however, lie the heavily-populated and semi-arid areas of the Mossi plateau, in many aspects an extension of the Sahel, which thus conditions much of the reality of people's lives and the constraints they face.

Throughout history, fate has dealt severely with the people of the Sahel, who inhabit some of the most dust-dry margins of the liveable earth. But today that fate is no longer in the hands of their great deity, Wende. Instead it is a secular fate, calculated in gross national product, debt servicing ratios, and infant mortality rates. And by all these yardsticks, Burkina Faso is one of the poorest countries in the world, many of its people malnourished, illiterate, and afflicted with all the ills that flesh is heir to. This, we are told, is the truth about Burkina. And there are plenty of statistics to prove it. You will find some of them in this book. Poverty, however, is only one dimension of life for the people of Burkina, and many expert foreign advisers have seen their grand projects founder because they came with only one-dimensional solutions to offer.

In the following pages, this account of development in Burkina Faso today tries to convey something of the conditions of life, the hopes and aspirations of its people, the conflicts they face and the never-ending struggles which many must endure in order to have any future at all. It focuses particularly on the Sahelian zone, because that is where people's lives and livelihoods are most directly under threat, and where both the government and foreign agencies have concentrated most of their development efforts. But there is an important caveat. This can only be a secular guide, mostly limited to tangible, measurable realities and the kind of thing that people are prepared to say to a stranger. And what a stranger feels in the Sahel, more strongly than most other places on earth, is the power of the unspoken, the impalpable. Between the lines, therefore, you must read many long silences, a lot of human warmth and laughter, a reverence for all the spirits that have been part of this world since time immemorial — and imagine above it all, from one flat horizon to the other, the great unbroken canopy of sky.

EMPIRES OF GOLD

As long ago as 6000 BC, Neolithic people of the Sahel began to discover agriculture. Tribes along the Niger valley cultivated sorghum, millet, some varieties of rice, fonio and sesame — the same crops as are grown there today. And in the rivers they fished with harpoons and nets. The climate at the time was kinder to them than now, with more rain and much thicker vegetation, but soon after came the long period of extreme drought which by 2000 BC had created the present Sahara desert. From then on, the Sahel has become slowly but progressively more arid.

A thousand years ago — at least a century or two before the Norman conquest of Britain — the people of the Sahel knew great wealth. In the year 970, the first recorded empire of West Africa, old Ghana, was described as 'the richest in the world because of its gold'. Founded by the Soninké people on the territory of present-day Mali and Mauritania, that empire boasted an army of 200,000 men, including 40,000 archers and an imposing cavalry. It reached its peak in the tenth century before succumbing to the advance of Islam from the North.

Two centuries later there arose the Empire of Mali, whose most celebrated emperor, Kankou Moussa, made a pilgrimage to Mecca in 1324, trekking across half the continent laden with gold and with an entourage of 60,000 people. Then, in the sixteenth century, it was the turn of the fabled city of Timbuktu to achieve renown, as the gateway for trans-Saharan trade and a university town with 25,000 students.

At about the same time, on the central plateau of what is now Burkina Faso, the Mossi people were consolidating their kingdoms, which were to last for another 400 years. The Mossi developed a highly-structured political system with precise customs and observances. There were five kingdoms, the most important in size and population being that of the emperor, the Mogho Naaba of Ouagadougou.

The power of the Mossi dynasty came to an end in 1896 in the reign of Naaba Wobgo, 'the Elephant Emperor', when the French marched in with a column of infantry to begin 64 years of colonial rule. In 1904 the Mossi lands were absorbed in the colony of Upper Senegal-Niger, before the new colony of Upper Volta was created in 1919, with borders similar to those of Burkina today.

A Touareg cattle herder at Djibo market, Soum province.
(Jeremy Hartley/Oxfam)

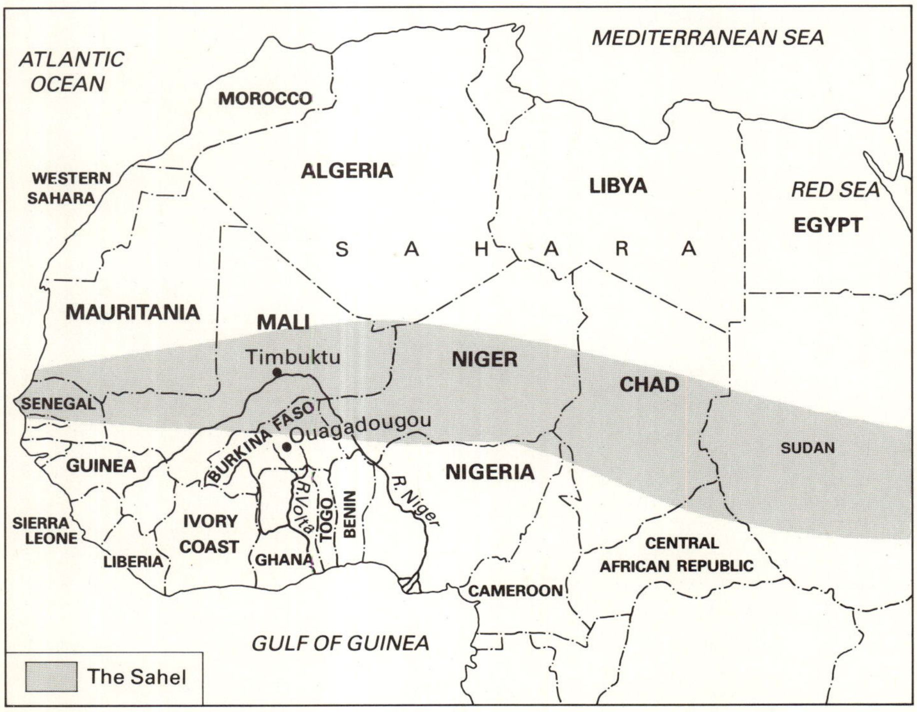

A RICH MOSAIC OF CULTURES

A Peul woman in Gorom-Gorom, Oudalan province.
(Jeremy Hartley/Oxfam)

Starting from the earliest times, waves of migration from north, south, east and west have made Burkina a melting-pot of languages and cultures. Among the country's nine million people there are no fewer than 60 ethnic groups, speaking at least 15 languages. The presence of some tribes — Gourounsi, Sénoufo, Dogon, Gourmantché, and Bwa — goes back into the mists of time. Over the centuries others arrived as invaders or refugees and were progressively assimilated. Then in the fifteenth century came the Mossi horsemen, probably riding north in search of new lands. In battle, they had the superiority of strong and speedy stallions; in conquest, the certainty of a divine right conferred by their all-powerful god, Wende; and in government, a gift for organisation to set the seal on their authority.

They soon subdued the original inhabitants of the central plateau region and established their kingdoms, which were to endure for four centuries. And throughout that time they fiercely resisted the advance of Islam, as Arab armies from the north overthrew the empires of neighbouring Mali and Niger. Today they remain the dominant ethnic group of Burkina Faso, accounting for about half the population. Other main groups are the Peul (Fulani), Lobi, Mandé, Bobo, Gourounsi, and Gourmantché people — but despite the diversity of language and culture, inter-marriage has been common and today there is little conflict between them.

The Mossi people are settled farmers, their society strongly patriarchal. The Peul tribe, on the other hand, with the nomadic Touaregs who invaded from the desert to the north, are the nation's herders. The ancestors of the Peuls are thought to have made their way here long ago from Ethiopia, 3,000 miles to the east. And in contrast again with the Mossi people, the Lobi tribe in the south west — like many from the forest zone of coastal west Africa — have a matriarchal society which gives their women a large degree of personal and social freedom.

A highly stratified society evolved in the Mossi kingdoms, with the royal family at the top of a pyramid consisting of many different castes: nobles, freemen, musicians and storytellers (*griots*), and slaves. As the political leader of his people, the Mossi emperor, the Mogho Naaba, had a large court of ministers, witch-doctors, entertainers, eunuchs and several hundred wives. At the same time he was and is the supreme religious leader, sharing the divinity of his forebears, who are traced back to the great common ancestor, Gbewa. On the death of an emperor, the chief of the *griots* was called upon to recite from memory the names and accomplishments of all past emperors: a symbolic linking of past and present. And although now restricted to his religious functions, the Mogho Naaba remains the embodiment of tribal authority, which is still a powerful force.

Amid the diversity of their cultures, the people of Burkina Faso — indeed of all the Sahel — hold certain fundamental customs and practices in common. Loyalty, first and foremost, is to one's clan or extended family, and then to one's native village. The family is the beginning and the end: its bonds are both practical (with a hierarchy through which the individual rises in each phase of life) and metaphysical, as embodied in religious observances at the family altar. It is the village, after that, which confers social identity — the framework within which each person learns his or her place in the world, is initiated into adulthood with age-old rituals, and establishes lifetime bonds with those of the same age group.

In both family and village, the traditional hierarchies have guaranteed for everyone a measure of security. As long as time stands still, there is everything to be said for equating age with wisdom. Government by the most elderly (gerontocracy) made sense in the Sahel for all the centuries that the essential rules of life remained unchanged.

For 30 years, the people of Burkina have watched as the high priests of development have preached sermons and distributed their multi-million dollar alms. But they see it has brought few blessings. They are poorer than before. A handful of middle men have got rich. The griot gives way to the transistor radio, and the sacramental rites of passage which were a unique bond between each person and their world, these too are on the road to extinction. And in return? Is a modern society, even if wished for, any nearer? Has the transfer of many powers to a younger generation opened new paths to advancement, to more democratic values? It would not be advisable to add up the pluses and minuses just yet.

But in less than 100 years the certainties which gave meaning to people's beliefs, which underpinned the social observances and the moral framework of their lives, have collapsed like a mudbrick wall under heavy rains. The first devastating shock was the imposition by France of a bureaucratic power structure, overriding the traditional systems of authority and respect, which, for the Burkinabè people, held everything else together. Then came colonial laws introducing private land-holding — an anathema to the local people — and attempts to introduce a money economy and modernise farming practices. Farmers were forced to introduce cash crops, needing money income to pay the poll tax levied on them.

A new era of migration then saw millions leaving their home country for paid jobs in the neighbouring French colonies and in Ghana. Most came back in due course, and their money and their new ideas began inevitably to erode the status quo. After independence in 1960, the alien concept of national statehood — in the hands of a privileged few protected by French patronage — deepened the divide between the people and their ruling elite. Then in the early 1970s came the drought, bringing with it not only hunger, destruction of land and crops, and decimation of their herds, but also in bewildering numbers that modern magician, the aid worker. A few carried Bibles, but most were proselytising for that even stranger creed called development. *Money and change equals progress*, it said. But when the little you possess has been won by attrition from the elements and has had to stand the most savage tests of time, 'development' and getting rid of well-tried old things can only seem an incomprehensible risk, if not sheer madness.

At the same time, gerontocracies are by their nature resistant to change, do stifle the ideas of the young, and do perpetuate inequalities — for example, the subordination of women. But this resistance to change has enabled the Mossi people, better than many other West Africans, to preserve their fundamental beliefs against the advances of the missionaries of Islam and, more recently, of Christianity. Over several hundred years, Islam has gained converts south of the Sahara, especially among the rich and powerful, but the mosques which are a feature of any village skyline in neighbouring Mali are much less in evidence here. Some two-thirds of the population adhere to their animist religion, while perhaps 30 per cent are nominally Moslem and 10 per cent Christian. Though often regarded dismissively by Europeans, animist beliefs reflect the spirituality of people who live in harmony with their natural environment. They speak of the essential unity of the visible and invisible worlds. Forces in the natural world are made known through the ancestors and can be used for good or evil: it is humanity which has the moral responsibility of choice. Living people are a continuation of the life stream of the first beings, and the ancestors are each person's intermediaries with the creator of the universe.

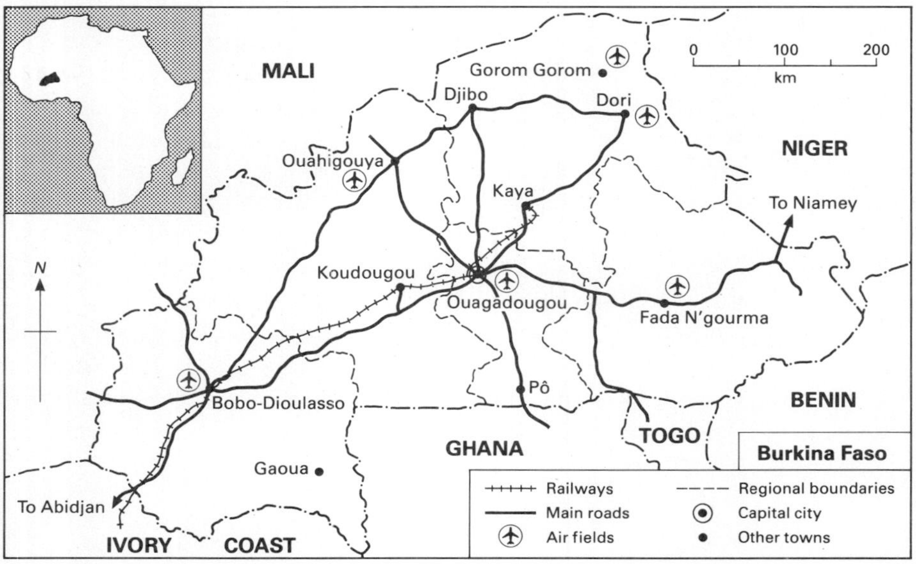

ARTS OLD AND NEW

ssaka Tapsoba with a statuette made y the 'lost wax' technique in his orkshop in Ouagadougou.
eremy Hartley/Oxfam)

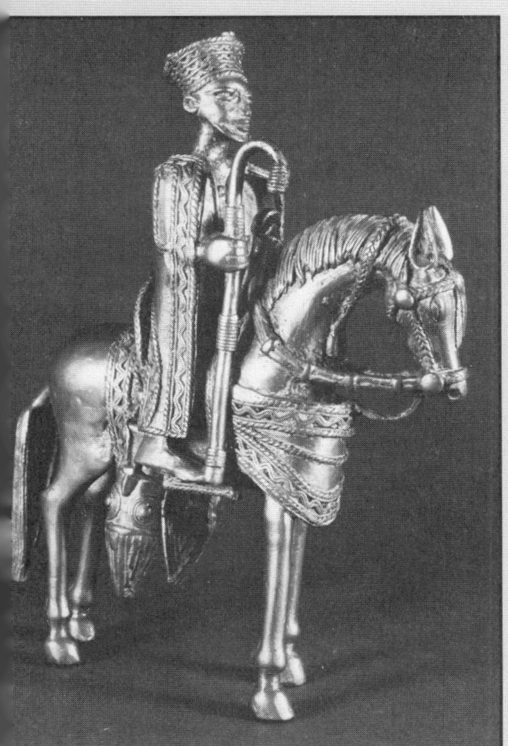

statuette of the Mogho Naaba, made the Tapsoba family workshop in uagadougou.
obert Davies/Oxfam)

Music and dance, body decoration, fine jewellery and costumes for the king's courtiers, folk tales and stories of magic passed down by word of mouth from generation to generation — these have been the traditional art forms of the Burkinabè people. Their culture is a complex weft of spiritual beliefs and social customs.

Each emperor of the Mossi tribe — the supreme religious leader — was immortalised with a statuette by the leading goldsmith-jeweller of his court. After completing this work, which was regarded as the peak of his achievement, the artist had to renounce his profession and go into retreat so as not to be tempted to reproduce it. Thus each emperor's statue was unique. For their intricately-decorated bronze bangles and other jewellery, these artists used the 'lost-wax' technique which is still a standard method of casting for sculptors today. Beautifully-modelled bronze statuettes are now produced in the workshops of Ouagadougou. Pieces costing anything from a few pounds to more than a thousand are displayed on street stalls, in craft shops or hotel boutiques.

The Tapsoba family work in a sculptors' collective, producing everything from ashtrays to splendid equestrian statues of the Mossi emperor, the Mogho Naaba, whose image is no longer sacrosanct. Clay for the moulds comes from a dam nearby; the beeswax for modelling is brought in from surrounding villages.

In the past few years, Burkina Faso has also rapidly acquired an international reputation in one of the principal artforms of the twentieth century — the cinema. With its Panafrican Cinema Festival (FESPACO) every two years, Ouagadougou has become 'the Hollywood of Africa' and Burkinabè directors are winning film prizes and appreciative audiences around the world. One of the best known, Idrissa Ouédraogo, was awarded a special prize at the 1989 Cannes Film Festival for his elegiac story of village life, *Yaaba* (The Grandmother), and he is already at work on another. Since 1986, despite all the problems of getting them financed and distributed, Burkina has been producing two full-length feature films a year.

(Mark Edwards/Oxfam)

DOWN WITH THE TOADIES!

'Down with imperialism! Down with the enemies of the people! Down with the embezzlers of public funds! Down with the toadies and thieving rats! Down with the predatory owls that strike in the darkness! Down with the fence-sitting chameleons! Down with the ravenous jackals! Down with the wreckers!'

Thomas Sankara, a young and charismatic army officer, was the man who made it his mission to transform Burkina Faso — or Upper Volta, as it was called until he renamed it in 1984. His aim was to bring his country out of the long shadows of poverty, dependence and feudalism. For a new generation of Africans, despairing of their exploitation by the imperialist world economy and by their own incompetent or corrupt leaders, Sankara's was a voice in the wilderness. His message to his own people, and to Africans everywhere, was that they should take destiny into their own hands, struggle proudly for their future, and reject domination or interference from any source, whether in their village, country or the world at large.

Sankara had a dazzlingly original line in revolutionary rhetoric, and his words resounded across the continent. He was hailed as a prophet of the people's liberation. At home, the revolution which brought him to power in 1983 set about dismantling both the old tribal power structures, deemed reactionary and obscurantist, and the privileges of the urban elite, which had become entrenched at the expense of the rural poor.

A village pharmacist in Sapone, Bazéga province. Nearly 300 dispensaries were built in the 18 months after the revolution in 1983.

(Jeremy Hartley/Oxfam)

'After a year and a half of revolution, we can pride ourselves on having constructed schools, clinics and dams, built roads, increased our farmland, and carried out reforestation. We can also take pride in having provided housing for the people. But this is not enough. Much more remains to be done. Most important is the effort we have made to transform people's attitudes. Each one of us now feels that wielding power is his business, that the destiny of Burkina Faso is the business not just of certain people but of all Burkinabès. Everyone has something to say. Each one of us demands an accounting from the other. Never again will things be done as before. No longer will the wealth of our country belong to a minority. This wealth belongs to the majority, a majority that speaks its mind.' (Thomas Sankara)

Before the revolution, 23 years of independence and a succession of governments — following policies largely prescribed by the French or other foreign advisers — had left Burkina in a sorry state. Political independence was fine for the educated elite who inherited the colonialists' mantle and who had learned the discreet charms and perquisites of power. But for the ordinary people, the rural poor, political independence meant little and brought less.

During the 1970s, agricultural output per person fell by 13 per cent. At the end of the decade, fewer than two people in a hundred had access to electricity. This was not a developing country. For the great majority, prospects of a decent life were shrinking year by year.

Political independence meant little to the ordinary people of Burkina, to begin with, because their concept of society had nothing to do with the modern nation-state. The governments of the 1960s and 1970s had shown no understanding of the need to create a new iconography, a new symbolic framework, as the basis for nation-building. But Thomas Sankara understood this very well. On the first anniversary of the revolution he gave his country a proud new name, a new anthem and a new flag. To underscore his commitment to radical changes giving power to the people, he himself maintained a spartan lifestyle. Sometimes he rode around Ouagadougou on a bicycle, played the guitar at mass rallies, or summoned ambassadors to present their credentials in a village, saying 'Tell *them* (the villagers) why you are here.'

The salaries of civil servants were slashed, officials were obliged to declare their personal wealth, and government ministers were allowed only a Renault 5 as their official car. The previous regime's fleet of Mercedes-Benz limousines were put up as special prizes in the national lottery.

The revolution sought to signal a new kind of independence — the liberation and progress of the people through their own efforts — but also, and more fundamentally, a new vision of society incompatible with the old. Sankara it was who inspired them with this vision and, at least for a little while, galvanised them into action. In less than 18 months, under the People's Development Programme, peasants and townspeople put their shoulders together and built over 300 schools, 280 dispensaries, 550 housing units and 260 dams, in addition to nearly 1,000 wells and boreholes. Available water supplies rose from under nine million tons in 1983 to 300 million tons in 1986.

From Day 1, to implement his programme of reforms, Sankara had created Committees for the Defence of the Revolution (CDRs) in every town and village throughout the country, eclipsing the traditional village chiefs. Many of these CDRs genuinely represented the will of the people, whose repressed energies were mobilised in projects for their own development. Others, however, with their kalashnikovs to enforce obedience, behaved arrogantly, made the people work for no payment, and were sometimes little better than bandits.

Impatient for change, Sankara issued policy edicts with little or no coherent planning, and alienated one by one the political and social forces which had backed the revolution. As his actions became more arbitrary, so he himself became more and more isolated. In retrospect, his downfall evokes all the inevitability of a Shakespearian tragedy: a good man challenging forces beyond his control, in this case the well-off town-dwellers — officials and merchants doing nicely as things were — and all the retinue of workers under their patronage.

Four years after he moved into the presidential palace, a flurry of anonymous pamphlets attacking Sankara began to circulate in Ouagadougou. A new struggle for power was under way. On October 15, 1987, the 37-year-old President and 12 of his closest aides were assassinated by the troops of his long-time friend and fellow officer, Blaise Compaoré. Shock waves reverberated around the country and far beyond. African heads of state who carried no particular torch for Sankara deplored his brutal elimination, and for some time the new President Compaoré found himself ostracised by many.

His first major task was one of national reconciliation: to regain the confidence and support of those organisations — political groups and trade unions in particular — which had turned against the revolution under Sankara's autocratic reign. Dialogue was the order of the day, including new talks with the World Bank and the International Monetary Fund, and overtures to personalities of the pre-revolutionary period, hitherto vilified as the running dogs of capitalism.

Compaoré's Popular Front replaced the National Revolutionary Council; unarmed Revolutionary Committees took over from the gun-toting CDRs. An uneasy calm returned to daily life. The people, their volatile hero in his grave, turned their backs once again on Ouagadougou: the plots and in-fighting between elite factions in the capital were essentially an irrelevance for them. As a gesture of disdain, the revolutionary rallying-cry *La patrie ou la mort, nous vaincrons* (The fatherland or death, we shall triumph) was mercilessly parodied. One variant: *La patrie ou l'amour, nous verrons* (The fatherland or love, we'll see).

The revolution, said Compaoré, would continue. But his policy of 'rectification', while undoubtedly redressing some of the excesses of the first four years, seemed to many a way of ditching the egalitarian principles which had provided its moral foundation. The other two 'historic leaders' of the revolution — Henri Zongo and Jean-Baptiste Lingani — were less than lukewarm about the President's distinct shift to the right in the name of consensus-building. Though retaining cabinet posts, they found themselves progressively excluded from policy-making after Sankara's death, yet they represented a potential opposition that Compaoré could not ignore.

In September 1989, Zongo and Lingani were arrested and summarily executed; it was alleged that they had plotted a coup. The ordinary Burkinabè could only shrug in resignation, noting meanwhile that Compaoré had just set up a new militia with the vague purpose of 'safeguarding the achievements of the revolution'. Towards the end of 1989, residents of Ouaga found themselves subject to new stop-and-search patrols.

While some commentators see the Compaoré regime as an improvement, not least economically, on what had gone before, others — at least until early 1990 — feared further repression of civil liberties. Then, however, the government announced the establishment of a consultative body to draw up a new Constitution, and a new law was passed to allow freer public debate in the media. These are encouraging signs, even though it is difficult to discern the overall thrust of government policies, as the World Bank, an important new influence in post-revolutionary Burkina, candidly admits: 'The likely future directions of the new policies are not clear,' it says. 'The present combination of militant ideology and pragmatism generates complex messages whose deeper meaning is not easy to decipher.'

While the outside world waits to see if Compaoré will long survive the three comrades-in-arms he has buried, the President himself is beset by no such doubts. A new presidential palace is now being built in Ouagadougou, costing something over £15 million.

Looking back on the Sankara years, Albertine Lankwandé, an official of the Burkina Women's Union in the province of Gourma, says, 'Sankara was devoted to his country, but his regime was too hard for us; the country is too poor and he jumped into too many things. As soon as one job was finished, we immediately had to start another. Contributions were demanded from the people for building a school or a cinema, but the people just didn't have the money. So Sankara was a hard task-master. He expected everyone to make sacrifices, but that's pretty difficult when you start with nothing.'

'Now it's our turn to have our say - the peasants of Burkina.' Roadside poster in Bobo-Dioulasso.
(Jeremy Hartley/Oxfam)

CAPITALISM WITH A MARXIST FACE

'Eat Burkinabè!' - a government poster in Bobo-Dioulasso urges self-sufficiency.
(Jeremy Hartley/Oxfam)

No wonder the World Bank is bemused. Here is a government declaring its commitment to a revolution founded on the principles of Marxism-Leninism, yet with a leader who says, 'We need a development of capitalism; for us it has never been a question of socialism.' To square the circle, the formula adopted by President Compaoré's Popular Front is a policy of 'state capitalism'. And the World Bank and IMF, in prescribing the economic medicine which Burkina will have to swallow to get some big development loans, seem prepared to take it on trust.

In fact, on the purely economic criteria of making ends meet, the country is in better shape than many others of sub-Saharan Africa. Though among the very poorest, it is one of the few to have notched up regular annual increases in national income, with growth since the revolution averaging 4.6 per cent a year. This is faster than the rise in population and compares with annual growth of 3.1 per cent over the preceding five years. In 1988 this represented an annual money income of about £135 a year for the average Burkinabè.

Foreign debt soared from US$134 million to $742 million in the decade to 1987, and debt repayment liabilities escalated almost tenfold to $50 million a year. But while this is not regarded as a serious problem by the World Bank, state revenue falls far short of government spending requirements, and the country has a huge trade gap. Exports, though rising healthily with big increases in gold and cotton sales, cover only half the cost of the country's imports. The trade deficit in 1987 reached more than £150 million.

But beyond the purely economic criteria of development, there is not much comfort. The new 'Human Development Index' published by the UN Development Programme in May 1990 — which ranks countries according to their people's literacy, life expectancy and purchasing power — finds Burkina third from bottom of the global league table. Out of 130 countries, only nearby Niger and Mali fare worse.

Thomas Sankara's National Revolutionary Council drew up a five-year development plan for 1986-90, with a budget of £1,200 million, of which a little over half would be spent on services such as transport, energy and water; 20 per cent for agriculture and livestock; 9 per cent on mining and manufacturing; 4.2 per cent on education and training; 3.2 per cent on health, and 2.5 per cent on housing. More than four-fifths of the money needed was expected to come from foreign sources, but in the first year less than half the funds available were actually spent: there simply weren't the trained staff needed to handle more than that.

Negotiating to introduce a Structural Adjustment Programme, the World Bank and the Burkina government insist that the country's economy is basically sound, and that very severe measures, which hit the poor hardest, will not be required. But it is not at all clear if the Bank's funds can be absorbed better than those of the Five-Year Plan.

There are two glaring omissions in the World Bank's two-volume report on Burkina, produced in 1989. First, and perhaps symptomatic of the post-Sankara mood, is the failure to consider the vital role of women in Burkina's economy. Second, in looking for ways to restructure government expenditure, the report makes no mention of the largest ministerial budget of all: defence. In 1989 the military government budgeted £40 million for defence — almost 20 per cent of its total resources, three times the allocation for health and nearly six times as much as for agriculture. To all this, the World Bank turns a blind eye.

How will structural adjustment affect the poorest people of Burkina? - Longa village, Yatenga province.
(Jeremy Hartley/Oxfam)

GETTING ORGANISED

Burkina is a great country for organisations. Visitors may be forgiven for thinking otherwise, because a large number of them don't actually work, but wherever a group of Burkinabès gather together around a particular problem, they will invariably set up an association, a committee or a co-operative to tackle it.

Most of the organisations which do work well for their members are in the rural areas. In town, the most visible — and frequently least effective — are either appendages of the government bureaucracy, or political or social groups serving above all the interests of those who control them.

On the other hand, a recent study in six of the country's 30 provinces found a 'remarkable dynamic' among village groups, with more than 3,800 associations in the 1,780 villages surveyed. A most notable feature of this phenomenon has been the growth of the Groupements Naam — groups based on a traditional Mossi form of young people's association for community work. In recreating the original Naam concept, the groups' founder, Bernard Lédéa Ouédraogo, introduced one innovation: he gave them economic objectives.

Each Groupement is normally directed by a management committee including men and women, although some groups are specifically for one sex or the other. The group as a whole decides on its objectives, while the committee looks after the management of funds, credit, community work sites and the appointment of an animator. In the past 12 years they have expanded rapidly, spreading from Yatenga, where they began, to 17 other provinces. They are closely linked with the Association Six-S, another brainchild of Mr Ouédraogo, which raises funds internationally to provide the village-level groups with the training, equipment and financial resources they need to push forward their development activities.

The Zemstaaba women's cooperative in Tanghin-Barrage, Ouagadougou. With a start-up loan from Oxfam, the group is earning money by rearing pigs, making baskets, and constructing slow-burning cookers for sale.
(Jeremy Hartley/Oxfam)

At the other end of the organisational spectrum stand Burkina's political parties. Under the Marxist banner of the revolution a strong Communist Party would be expected. But Burkina manages to have no fewer than six Communist parties, each with a distinct interpretation of the Marxist message, and each at loggerheads with the others most of the time. Until recently other parties were banned. So the intellectual elites in Ouagadougou could indulge themselves with a wide range of political choice: any colour they liked so long as it was red. Now, however, the Popular Front has opened its doors to two non-Communist parties as well.

Somewhere between the politicians and the peasants come all the organisational ganglia of the government bureaucracy. Each Ministry, it seems, is busy setting up a new Office for this, a new Service for that, a new Unit for the other. All eminently desirable and admirably planned; it's just that many of them lack the basic staff or equipment actually to do the job intended.

Decentralising government functions to the provinces should be an excellent idea, but too often the result, in practice, is a lot of city bureaucrats-in-exile trying to do too much with too little. On top of this, the rural government agent is sometimes unsuitable for the job, possibly fed up at being banished to the bush, and can therefore seem, in the eyes of the local people, more trouble than he's worth.

These shortcomings, however, do not imply anything basically wrong with the organisational strategy. Though Burkina's rural extension workers have been better paid, trained and equipped than many in surrounding countries, the problem remains essentially one of inadequate means, coupled with a need for better co-ordination between agencies.

TRADE UNIONS: A FORCE TO BE RECKONED WITH

In most of Africa, the trade union movement has little independence and less clout. But Burkina is different. Here, individual unions thrive and are an important element of the nation's political life (in the cities, at least).

The teachers' union, closely linked to a political party associated with one of the pre-revolutionary regimes, was the first to come out in opposition to the Sankara government. When their leaders were arrested in March 1984, the teachers went on strike. The government retaliated by firing 2,600 of them. Initially, the Confederation of Burkinabè Unions supported the revolution, but soon changed its mind. By early 1985 there was a broad Trade Union Front denouncing the government for 'the constant worsening of the disastrous conditions of life of the working masses'.

In the context of African politics, Burkina's trade unions may indeed hold an unusual if not unique place on the national scene. For one thing, they are now the only people's movement outside the Popular Front. But the working masses they claim to represent are in reality no more than a small minority, consisting almost entirely of salaried urban workers.

The conflict between Sankara and the trade unions intensified from 1985, with many union leaders arrested and tortured. Was this a factor in his downfall? All that is known is that Blaise Compaoré began to distance himself from Sankara's bitter campaign before the coup and has since sought to bring the unions back into the fold.

It may appear one of the ironies of the revolution that the trade unions have been rehabilitated under a regime dedicated to 'state capitalism', after being hounded under one ostensibly committed to supporting the workers through class struggle. But for Sankara, 'the workers' meant the 90 per cent of his people living in the rural areas, while under Compaoré the centre of political gravity has reverted to the cities, where the unions can play their power games. It's really all quite logical.

THE ENVIRONMENTAL CHALLENGE

To journey across the Sahelian provinces — Yatenga, Soum, Oudalan and Seno — is to enter a world that is almost mesmeric in its timelessness, its seeming emptiness; a world also to be wondered at for the grandeur of its long, slow dying. A barren landscape of thin yellow grass and gravel, interspersed with the spreading patches of dead skin which is desertification. The skeletons of trees stand like contorted crosses in a graveyard where the battle for survival has been fought and lost. Carcasses of giant baobab trees, like fallen warriors, lie toppled on the scorched earth. The desolation is almost breathable.

On the dirt road, now and then, a solitary person appears, far from anywhere, walking, cycling, perhaps pushing a dead motorbike, carrying a waterpot. They seem lost figures walking into eternity: for miles further on, having overtaken them, one finds no destination to which they could conceivably have been heading.

In 20 years of drought and deforestation, many villages of the Sahel have lost a third, sometimes as much as half, of their cultivable land. And 'lost' is not just a euphemism: in the dry season, from November to May, hot, abrasive easterly winds lift millions of tons of precious topsoil from the now denuded terrain, carrying it westwards to fall uselessly in the Atlantic Ocean. And from June to October, when the rain does come, it often comes in torrents, and where little plant life remains to protect it, the soil is washed away into gulleys and rivers.

Not only in the Sahel but throughout the more populous, semi-arid regions of the country, the land is under threat. The centuries-old equilibrium between man and nature has broken down under a combination of stresses. Apart from rising populations and a slow but progressive drying of the climate, one of the main factors is the disintegration of the survival strategies of rural societies, caused in turn by factors as diverse as the country's foreign debt and the introduction of cash crops.

The threat of drought and famine has been a condition of life in the Sahel since the earliest times. We know of terrible famines lasting several years in each of the last three centuries. But the drought which began in 1968, and which continued with only brief periods of remission for almost 20 years, has seen the precarious balance between people and nature wrecked almost beyond repair. It is not that tens of thousands of people died of hunger and thirst; it is not that their herds were decimated; for in earlier times this could have been regarded as the harsh price for maintaining an equilibrium between human activities and what the fragile earth could sustain. The crisis now is at once brutally simple and infinitely complex. It poses essentially one question: with the land overworked and dying, with more people than ever competing to scratch a living from it and in desperation ignoring their own time-honoured codes for conserving their natural resources, and with few hopes of climatic change in their favour, what possible transformation can offer a future for these people and their earth?

In the past, the Gourounsi people in the south of Burkina were particularly careful in managing their environment. Their elders included a Chief of the Greenwood, whose job was to protect the forests and to ensure that valuable species were not felled. But today, that concern is being overtaken by other demands on land use. And when people from some other place are liable to come in their trucks to chop down your trees, there may be no other viable strategy for poor villagers than to get in first.

Elsewhere, the fatal process of deforestation continues unabated. Bushfires, it is estimated, blacken as much as 50,000 square kilometres — one-fifth of the country's land area — every year. Most are set deliberately to clear land for agricultural expansion or to encourage new grazing;

'Years ago the land around our village was forest. There were many wild animals — lions, panthers, buffalo, elephant, antelope and a lot more. But now there is almost no wildlife, and very few trees.' — Guiro Mahama, president of Goumba village group, Yatenga

The lions and elephants have gone, but poisonous snakes remain. Guiro Mahama, of Goumba village, Yatenga province, examines a specimen.
(Jeremy Hartley/Oxfam)

The desert creeps across Yatenga province, northern Burkina.
(Mark Edwards/Oxfam)

sometimes also because it is the traditional belief that fire can purge evil spirits at the New Year. Combined with the country's fuelwood consumption of 5 million cubic metres a year, these factors provide some measure of the deforestation problem.

While other countries of the Sahel are no less threatened by this kind of environmental bankruptcy, Burkina is widely regarded as the most progressive in its efforts to tackle the crisis. Key to the government's policy has been a three-pronged campaign against bushfires, against illegal woodcutting, and against the uncontrolled grazing of livestock. Enforcement of this policy under Sankara was tough, but by 1989 the sanctions against offenders had been relaxed. Repressive measures, explained the then Environment Minister Beatrice Damiba, were no substitute for awareness-raising: 'The struggle against desertification is a long-term one. The first necessity is to convince the people of the rightness of what one wants them to do.'

Traditional rights of property, sustainable for as long as the people-to-land ratio remained low, have been deemed an obstacle to rational land use which also contributes to the deterioration of soils. There are three types of land-holding under the traditional system: a family's collective hereditary right to land, which any member of that family may exploit; a priority right of the village chief to certain lands held by him as a symbol of the compact between his people and the supernatural powers of the earth; and usage rights, permanent or temporary, which may be assigned to a group or individual.

Over the past century, as emigration drained increasing numbers of workers from the family fields, the practice of land-lending became widespread. But because tree-planting had traditionally been a mark of land ownership, it was a condition of such loans that the tenant should not plant trees or make other improvements. So the land suffered. Altogether, the system has become less and less able to cope with change and competing land-use pressures. Under the colonial administration, things were further complicated by laws introducing the alien concept of private property, designed not least to enable the colonists to obtain an outright title to land.

Oxfam's spirit-level in action: two gradated poles and a transparent plastic tube filled with water enable farmers to find the contour lines on an apparently flat field.

(Jeremy Hartley/Oxfam)

At independence, therefore, Burkina inherited a dual system, which is still in place. The government has been preparing a fundamental land reform designed to permit nationwide land-use planning as a basis for promoting food self-sufficiency and housing development. Proposed legislation will make all land ultimately the property of the government. In the area of each village, zones will be demarcated for housing, agriculture, livestock, and forest land. But many peasants are hostile to these plans, some fearing that the zoning regulations will dispossess them, others that government ownership will leave their villages no sacred ground for the *chefs de terre* (land chiefs) to observe their traditional rites — on which depend, according to custom, their prospects of a good harvest.

Meanwhile, land reform or no, many thousands of villagers are now taking the future into their own hands and finding they can hold out hopes to their children which they thought were lost for ever. By the year 2000, it might just be possible to look back and see these faint sparks of energy and hope as the start of a renaissance for the Sahel.

'Now we are dynamic and determined to go ahead,' says Guiro Mahama, the village group president in Goumba, a thatched-hut settlement in the dry scrub of Yatenga province. 'You can't help a man who is asleep, but we are awake, and determined to progress.'

Is there any evidence to justify such hopes against what look like overwhelming odds? So far it remains scattered in the villages like Goumba where a few people have decided, mostly on their own initiative, to join together in practical measures to rebuild their lives and livelihoods. But the evidence from these communities, including some of the poorest in the land, shows that it's working — and generally with no more than a little stimulus of outside help from overseas voluntary agencies who, unlike the big, multi-million dollar aid donors, are the only ones able to think small, the only ones who start by designing projects in consultation with the people themselves.

Constructing a 'diguette': a line of stones laid along a contour line will catch rain water and reduce soil erosion.

(Jeremy Hartley/Oxfam)

That is the testimony from an increasing number of community-based initiatives undertaken by Burkina's own development groups such as the Naam, and by overseas agencies like Oxfam: helping to build small-scale dams to give local communities an assured water supply; helping pastoralists to rebuild herds depleted by the drought; providing start-up funds to women's groups so they can launch income-earning schemes and feed their families better. Perhaps most dramatically of all, with the simplest kind of grassroots technology, they have enabled villages all over Burkina to transform a traditional but not very efficient method of water conservation into one that is bringing their land back to life.

It all started around 1979 with a small Oxfam experiment in Yatenga, building low U-shaped earth walls to catch rainwater for tree seedlings planted inside them. The peasants who tried them were impressed, but were more interested in using the technique to grow food crops. Within a couple of years, developing a traditional method of their own, they were constructing low barriers of stones, stalks and branches across their fields to halt the water run-off.

At that stage, the main drawback was that on their usually very flat lands it was impossible to discern the contour lines on which the stone lines needed to be built in order to be fully effective. Here again, the Oxfam team came up with a brilliantly simple answer: a transparent, water-filled tube attached at each end to a vertically-held pole. With the poles placed a certain distance apart, they will be on the same contour when the water is at the same level in each end of the tube. Illiterate peasants can be taught how to use these water-levels in a two-day course.

From that point on, Oxfam's *Projet Agro-Forestier* — PAF for short — took off by leaps and bounds. Of more than 100 Oxfam projects in Burkina, it has become the best known and the most closely studied. In 1981, the stone lines or *diguettes* had been built on only seven hectares; by

1987, farmers had installed them on 1,200 hectares, the project was buying plastic tubing by the kilometre for water-levels, and a continuous stream of visitors was coming to learn how it was done. Nationwide, with adoption of this technique by the government and other aid agencies, the area of land treated now exceeds 5,000 hectares.

By increasing water penetration of the hard ground, the diguettes quickly proved they could reduce erosion, improve crop yields by up to 40 or 50 per cent, and recover totally degraded land. In one test undertaken by farmers themselves, it was found that where there were no stone lines, the soil level dropped four inches in a single year; but where they had been built, the soil level rose six to eight inches.

In the village of Baszaido, three years after the first diguettes were built, the contrast between land so treated and the rest is remarkable. Within the stone lines there is tall grass everywhere and a good harvest of ripening sorghum. On the other side of the path, a large expanse of barren ground. In another village, Ranawa, trees which were dying are recovering as the soil retains more moisture, and because the water table is replenished with rain penetrating the ground, wells which had dried up are giving water again.

Noogo village, Yatenga province: eucalyptus trees planted behind a diguette.

(Jeremy Hartley/Oxfam)

The PAF technique is extremely cheap, which accounts for the fact that it has now spread from Yatenga to more than half the provinces of the country, adopted widely by the government's extension service and by other voluntary organisations. Thousands have now been trained and news of the amazing results achieved with the diguettes continues to spread by example from village to village.

In recent times, under the direction of Yatenga-born Mathieu Ouédraogo, PAF has evolved a more integrated package of measures, which includes sowing live hedges and tree seedlings, digging compost pits, and constructing enclosures for goats. Considered a more sustainable approach than the stone lines on their own, this package, project workers hope, will be adopted as widely as the original scheme.

It would be wishful to imagine that small-scale innovations such as this could herald a renaissance for the battered Sahel. For every spark of hope there remain a dozen potential disasters that could snuff it out. In Goumba village, it is that spark, none the less, that keeps Guiro Mahama going and gives him a new confidence for tomorrow.

Vatering neem and eucalyptus seed-ings in a tree nursery run by the Ministry of Environment in Ouahigouya, Yatenga province. Oxfam's PAF team distributes the plants to distant villages.
Jeremy Hartley/Oxfam)

RECORD CROPS – NOT ENOUGH TO EAT

Production of the main staple crops, millet and sorghum, beat all records in 1988, and in good years the country is now reckoned to be fully self-sufficient in cereals. Food production overall grew by more than 7 per cent a year in the period 1983-87, well over double the rate of population growth and in striking contrast with the negative food trends in sub-Saharan Africa as a whole.

That represents a big improvement in the past ten years, even though it hides wide disparities in the amount that people in different income groups and different parts of the country can actually obtain.

Food aid makes up for some of the inequalities of distribution, but Burkina is still short of fruit, vegetables, meat and fish. Malnutrition is widespread, and the United Nations estimates that the country's overall food consumption is 14 per cent less than the minimum required for good health. Children are malnourished, in particular, because their families cannot afford an adequate diet, but also because of traditional eating habits and the lack of nutrition education for mothers. Food aid, though a necessary stop-gap to prevent famine in times of acute drought, is not a solution. Often it arrives too late, and, equally seriously, it depresses local farm prices, so that farmers in some areas give up growing the staple cereals and shift instead to cotton or other non-essential crops which are more remunerative. The net effect is likely to reduce food security. In 1988, the government wanted to buy up the cereal surplus of 42,000 tons from farmers, with the intention of storing and re-selling it at a modest mark-up in the hungry season before the next harvest. But it would have required a budget of £4 million and a massive logistical operation. In the end, the private merchants got there first, offering a higher purchase price. But as always, their re-sale mark-up, when people's own supplies ran out, would be several times the government margin, leaving the poor without the means to buy enough for their needs.

Selling millet from a village grain bank (funded by Oxfam) in Passoré province.
(Jeremy Hartley/Oxfam)

Progress towards food self-sufficiency was a principal objective of the Five-Year Plan for 1986-90. The strategy was based on targets for increasing production, raising peasant incomes, cutting the trade deficit attributable to food imports, and reducing the risk of crop failures through improved management of water supplies. Among other things, the Plan aimed to promote more intensive production techniques — the traditional hoe being still the only agricultural tool in general use — and more training and extension support for the mass of peasant farmers. Its authors can point to some successes. Cereal production, as noted above, has risen encouragingly. Though only one-third of the rural population has access to clean water, a big effort to improve water supplies has seen scores of small dams being built, providing some irrigation and water for animals. Also, in the first two years of the Plan, some 4,000 new wells and boreholes were dug, cutting substantially the distance that many women had to walk to fetch water.

Longa village, Yatenga province: preparing the ground for planting millet and beans.
(Jeremy Hartley/Oxfam)

CHANGING PATTERNS ON THE LAND

'My father had a huge herd of animals. We were particularly rich in cows and employed several herders to guard them. I knew nothing but the taste of milk and meat. Today I have forgotten the taste of that life. Now all those animals are dead and I am forced to live solely from farming.

'Over the last few years I have watched the landscape change in the most dramatic fashion. It has all passed before my eyes as if I were watching a film with a bad ending. We have not been able to reconstitute the herds which were almost wiped out by the drought. Animals are just about finished here.' — Hamadou Namoudou, Saouga village, Ouadalan province

(Jeremy Hartley/Oxfam)

While Burkina's farmers have for generations been able to trust their simple,time-tested methods of cultivation, the winds of change are now blowing unremittingly across their land. And for many nomadic or semi-nomadic pastoralists it has been that much harder, bringing to an end an age-old way of life which was the only way of making sustainable use of land on the arid Saharan fringe. Sustainable it was, but no more — at least only for a rapidly diminishing number. Too little rain, too many people and animals, whose overall numbers in the Sahel increased in spite of the ravages of drought: all in all, too many stresses for the land to bear. And on top of this, pastoralists have found themselves having to compete in their traditional markets of Ghana and Ivory Coast with subsidised frozen beef imported from Argentina. Increasingly, herders find they have no option but to renounce the nomadic life and pick up a hoe for the first time in their family's history.

In the northern provinces also, a traditional pattern of inter-dependence between nomadic herders and settled farmers is breaking down. The nomads would receive straw for their animals, in return for bringing their herds to fertilise the farmers' fields. But the farmers are being encouraged to go in for mixed farming themselves, with livestock to provide manure for their land, so they now want the straw for their own animals. Conflicts have also arisen as the farmers have bit by bit taken over areas previously used for grazing. The herders find themselves increasingly hemmed in, and although they still account for 30 per cent of the country's official export earnings, their share of national income is down from one-fifth in the 1970s to one-eighth now.

In the south west, meanwhile, a massive campaign by international agencies over several years has effectively eradicated river blindness, a disease which had kept population levels low and discouraged inward migration from other parts of the country. As a result, another wave of migration from the north has been opening up these new, fertile lands. But when food harvests are good, these farmers have found, there is no way to get their surpluses to market, even when other parts of the country, their crops blighted by locusts or inadequate rains, may be in desperate need. So many farmers have switched to growing cotton, which — because it earns valuable foreign exchange — the government will collect and buy at a guaranteed price. The south west is now Burkina's main cotton-producing region, and the impact of this development of the new lands is evidenced by the doubling of the country's cotton output between 1985 and 1988: from 85,000 tons to 176,000 tons in just three years.

Those figures look encouraging, and they are exactly the kind highlighted by the World Bank or the IMF when they seek to convince African governments that their economic salvation depends on strategies to promote exports. Unfortunately, there is another side to the story. The terms of trade for Africa's primary commodity exports, despite some fluctuation, have generally declined over the past 30 years. The rich world consumes more and more of Africa's produce, and pays steadily less in real terms for it. In the case of cotton, 10,000 tons sold at the world market price in January 1984 would have earned Burkina about US$19 million. Five years later, to earn the same amount the country had to sell 13,750 tons — and that makes no allowance for inflation. So just to keep income static, the cotton crop has to take up more precious land each year. For most of Africa, the diminishing returns of export-based economic strategies can only be averted by a drastic mortgaging of their natural resources. And if that is the best the rich world can recommend, its citizens must be prepared to understand — and either accept or fight — the consequences of human misery that it entails.

THE FARMERS' FUTURE

Almost 90 per cent of Burkina's people live off the land, so the future of farming is critical for the country's development. The government recognises this, even if it doesn't invest a great deal of money in agriculture; and the World Bank sees agriculture-related activities as the mainstay of the economy for the foreseeable future. So what are the prospects?

Many possibilities of change and modernisation could be cited, but most are highly uncertain. Three trends are worth mentioning, of which two could, in theory, radically improve Burkina's primary sector economy. The first trend is a changing attitude to farm investment in the more prosperous areas. In one of the richer cotton and cereal-growing areas, one-quarter of all farms now have animal-drawn ploughs, and their output in the past five years has increased dramatically. The power of example, spreading from village to village, could in time work the transformation which many expensive aid projects, intended to introduce farm mechanisation, have failed to achieve. Against this, however, is the fact that increases in output have largely been achieved by expanding the areas under cultivation, rather than by improved yields per hectare. And studies elsewhere in Burkina have shown that farmers with animal-drawn ploughs get only minimal increases in production, sometimes not enough to repay the cost of the plough.

A second hopeful area is the improvement of traditional crop varieties to increase yields and to make them more resistant to drought and pests. A number of improved sorghum varieties have been developed and adopted by farmers, but so far researchers have been unable to produce any millets capable of performing better than local varieties under the harsh conditions of the Sahel. In the longer term, it is an open question whether biotechnology may come up with altogether new kinds of crops suitable for the world's dry and semi-arid regions. So far, it seems that biotech salvation is only for those who can pay a high price for their indulgences — and who can hold out the promise of rich markets to make it worthwhile for the agribusiness multinationals to invest in the research. Burkina, and the Sahel in general, are unlikely to be able to buy such favours.

Perhaps the best bet, though by no means radical, is the third scenario: a continuing multiplication across the country of small village self-help schemes to restore the land, to make the best of the erratic rains, to plant crops again where for years nothing would grow, to put trees back on the denuded landscape: in short, to create the conditions where people can start to think about tomorrow. It may sound facile to a westerner's ear, but thinking about tomorrow is a luxury unknown to most people of the Sahel until the present generation. Once realised and — PAF! — all manner of unthinkable things emerge into the realm of the possible. In the three Sahelian provinces of Oudalan, Seno and Soum, for example, a significant number of associations of village groups has emerged. There are now over 400 village groups in these provinces, and they are said to represent as much as 80 per cent of the people.

Ploughing in Ranawa village, Yatenga province.
(Jeremy Hartley/Oxfam)

An empty granary in Dawanagomde village, near Ouagadougou.
(Jeremy Hartley/Oxfam)

THERE ARE NO SIGNPOSTS...

... to the village of Dawanagomde. A collection of huts buried in the bush a day's walk from the capital, Dawanagomde looks depressed — an impression confirmed in conversation with Mr Jeanny Tapsoba, president of the village group.

The settlement is said to be about 200 years old, but it's apparent that not much has happened in that time to improve the lives of its inhabitants. At present, Mr Tapsoba told us, things are going from bad to worse. First, they have a big problem with water: there is only one well, which is just not enough for their needs, and each year it dries up months before the rains come. The soil has become very poor, and crop yields are therefore declining. Food from this year's harvest wouldn't last long and the villagers expected to face six months of real hardship after that. Some of them knew a bit about vegetable gardening, but without water there was no chance of trying that.

There was a lot of illness in the village, he added, but at least there was a health post now where they could buy some medicines. In the past they had built diguettes of earth to retain water in the rainy season, but without any technical assistance they didn't work well. One ray of hope was a project to help them construct better stone diguettes, being organised by a local voluntary agency, FONADES. That, they hoped, would put life back into their badly eroded land and enable them to grow more food and escape the annual nightmare of the hungry season.

There wasn't much else to look forward to, except, for the children perhaps, Mr Tapsoba's nightly literacy classes. He gives them free, and the children sit on the ground or on a classroom bench under a thatch-roofed shelter, while Mr Tapsoba writes on a big blackboard. His handwriting is very neat. For Dawanagomde, his lessons and the new diguettes are perhaps their only claim on the future.

FAMINE EARLY WARNING

Every month in the three Sahelian provinces most vulnerable to food emergencies, a team of researchers monitors the conditions in eight selected villages. This is the *Système d'Alerte Précoce (SAP)*, a famine early-warning system which since 1987 has been giving the government regular reports on food supply prospects.

The researchers monitor rainfall, food stocks, crop development during the growing season, animal health, the condition of pasture and water-points for livestock, market prices, and the movement of people. Apart from written reports, radio can be used to give Ouagadougou urgent warning of events such as locust attacks.

In October 1989, at harvest time, the news from SAP was bleak. In some departments, they estimated, the harvests would be disastrous, giving only 20-30 per cent of normal yields. The damage had been done by a demoralising string of adversities unique to the Sahel: a plague of grasshoppers, birds, erratic and insufficient rains, a parasitic weed called *striga*, and an insect that kills millet by burrowing into the stalks.

Combining the stocks they had in hand with the new season's miserable crop, SAP Co-ordinator Julien Compaoré told us, many people would have enough food for barely six months. The next harvest was twelve months away. And the only reason they had any stocks at that point was that last year's food aid arrived six months too late. The Early Warning System could do nothing about that, he pointed out, and a lot of people went hungry as a result. Would the aid now urgently needed arrive on time this year?

Locusts are a problem all over the Sahel. In Goumba village, Yatenga province, farmers had to sow millet four times in one year, and each time the crop was destroyed.
(Jeremy Hartley/Oxfam)

SARATA WISHES SHE COULD BAKE SOME CAKES

Heavily pregnant with her sixth child, Mrs Sarata Sawadogo was working in the fields, helping to harvest the millet crop. She didn't mind taking a break to sit down and talk.

Sarata is 34 years old. She was born in the nearby village of Boulouga and came here to Longa when she was married. She has five children — four boys and a girl — and the oldest is now 11. Things had changed a lot, she said, since she came here. Then, there weren't so many people and there was more to eat. The biggest hardship now was the shortage of food, and 'if one is hungry, one is always ill'.

Longa has a population of 670. Sarata lives with 40 others in her husband's family compound. She has three fields and grows millet, beans and sorghum. The land used to be rich, but is now exhausted. She gets only a meagre crop.

The average Burkinabè woman works 16-18 hours a day, and Sarata is no exception. Like most, her day begins with a strenuous session of pounding millet for the family's meal, then she fetches water and after that there's an expedition of maybe eight kilometres to collect firewood, before returning home to prepare the midday meal. In the afternoon she goes to work in the fields with her husband, after which another session of pounding millet and another trip to the well for water. In the evening there are domestic chores such as cleaning and mending the children's clothes.

If she had one wish for herself, Sarata said, she would like to be able to afford the ingredients to make cakes and biscuits, which she could sell in the village. That way she'd be able to earn a little money to buy things she needed for her family — but for the moment that was out of reach. For the village as a whole, the best thing of all would be a small grinding mill. That would save all the women the arduous daily job of pounding grain into flour for their meals.

Goumba village, Yatenga province: Mrs Sarata Sawadogo grinding millet into flour to make tô for the evening meal.
(Jeremy Hartley/Oxfam)

TÔ WITH EVERYTHING

A stiff white porridge made of millet flour, tô is the centrepiece of the Burkinabè diet. It is served with a variety of sauces made from meat, fish, sesame seeds, okra or baobab leaves. For those who can afford it, meals may also include yams, cassava or sweet potatoes, boiled or fried, while protein is provided by peanuts and cowpeas. The seeds of the shea nut yield oil and margarine. Apart from those living on urban salaries, meat and fish are mostly reserved for special occasions.

Zoumkoom is a common drink, made from ground millet, water and the juice of the tamarind fruit. For something stronger there is the universal *dôlo*, a home-brewed millet beer, or bottled beer from one of Burkina's two breweries. Only women brew dôlo and many women in Ouaga, if they are using traditional stoves, need more than one ton of firewood a week to keep their pots bubbling.

In polygamous households, it is the husband who draws up the roster of food preparation for his wives. The rule is that the woman who prepares the food also spends the night with him.

Hot meals are usually prepared two or three times a day, but increases in the price of firewood force many poor families in urban areas to reduce this to once a day. In a household of six people, firewood may cost up to £9 a month, nearly one-third of their average income.

THE ROAD TO PROSPERITY?

For any country to make economic progress, it must find ways to produce a steady supply of tradeable goods or services. Some Third World countries have achieved rapid industrialisation in the past 25 years, but for the people of the Sahel this road to prosperity has proved to be another pot-holed track across the desert. Manufacturing industries accounted for 14 per cent of Burkina's national income in 1973, and 15 years later had still made no advance.

Centred largely on the processing of agricultural raw materials, the manufacturing sector is dominated by five parastatal enterprises handling cotton, sugar, edible oils, textiles, and flour. But the industrial sector as a whole, which counts about 200 companies, provides jobs for only about two per cent of Burkina's workforce. There has been hardly any foreign industrial development in the past 20 years.

The disincentives are all too evident. No industry can succeed without customers, and no more than a handful of Burkinabès have the cash to buy any goods which industry might produce. And, given the existing costs of labour, production and transport, there is little prospect of the manufacturing sector becoming competitive in export markets.

Two bright spots, at least in terms of giving a boost to Burkina's export figures since the mid-1980s, are cotton and gold. Gold sales quadrupled in the period from 1982 to 1987. But one of the most significant elements in sustaining the country's economy is the so-called 'informal sector' — that realm of small businesspeople, traders, artisans and pedlars who survive and thrive outside the formal economy by avoiding government regulations and taxes.

Noting that the informal sector produces more than 40 per cent of value-added in manufacturing, not to mention its significant role in agriculture and services, the World Bank has recommended that steps be taken to support and expand it. While it admits that 'informal-sector activities are commonly (and not without reason) equated with smuggling', the Bank says they play 'an essential role in development of the country's industrial fabric, employment creation and economic development in general'. In fact, informal sector trade between Sahelian countries — circumventing tariffs, paperwork and other controls — is estimated to exceed official trade by a substantial margin: often two or three times as much in volume and sometimes (notably in the case of gold smuggling) ten times.

Looking at the prospects for long-term industrialisation, the World Bank suggests that Burkina could aim to be competitive internationally either by thoroughly developing one or two product lines — processing and packaging fruit, meat or vegetables, for example — or by focusing its efforts on particular services, either health, tourism, data processing, telecommunications, banking, or training.

Although efforts are being made to extend tourist facilities, Burkina seems unlikely to improve rapidly on its current level of about 5,000 visitors a year. But given the poor state of services such as banking and communications in several neighbouring countries, the World Bank's suggestions are not as far-fetched as they might appear at first glance.

The remote north east region is thought to hold large deposits of manganese (as much as 17 million tons), but Northern financiers will not invest money in its extraction, doubting that it would be economically viable at current and projected world prices.

Lobi pottery on sale in Gaoua, near Bobo-Dioulasso.
(Jeremy Hartley/Oxfam)

DÔLO: THE REAL THING

Antoinette Bancé lives in the Goughin district of Ouagadougou and has made a name with her production of dôlo, Burkina's home-brewed millet beer. Now in her fifties, she has developed the business in the footsteps of her mother and her grandmother before her.

'Apart from eating, sleeping and looking after the health of my family,' says Antoinette, 'the rest of my time is devoted to the dôlo. That means buying the millet, germinating and drying it, grinding it and preparing the beer, then selling it, washing and rinsing the pots and calabashes. All this doesn't get done in a day! It needs careful planning.'

Known as 'AB' to her friends, she has a regular clientele and four women to help her. As well as the customers who come to drink on the premises, Antoinette supplies her dôlo wholesale to a number of other women, who sell it in town. She buys wood by the truckload and brews twice a week on an improved stove with four huge pots.

'The customer is king, so it's my job to make sure I provide a dôlo that is pure and of good quality. There are no additives in my beer. The only thing I do is to make sacrifices each year with a chicken, to thank the ancestors and to ask them to protect and bless me.'

Her daughters, however, have no intention of following Antoinette in the dôlo business. 'That's the problem with town girls,' she shrugs. 'They think it's too much like hard work.'

Women's business: brewing dôlo (beer made from millet).
(Mark Edwards/Oxfam)

A COFFEE-STALL IN DORI

Demo Mamoudou is 17 and already has several years' experience of making a living in the informal economy. He lives with his family in Dori, the dusty capital of Seno Province in the Sahelian zone, where his father is a livestock dealer. He has one brother and two sisters.

Demo went to school until he was 10. After that he got a job in a motor mechanic's shop, where he earned the equivalent of 40-50 pence a day. Now, serving on a coffee stall in one of Dori's main streets, next to the bus station, he says he can earn up to £1.00 a day and sometimes more. If indeed his take-home pay comes to five pounds a week, that's already double the income of the average Burkinabè.

On the morning we visited him, Demo had bought 40 small baguettes of French bread, and by eight o'clock all but four of them had been sold. This represented a profit of about 40 pence. He had also sold some 40 glasses of milk, making a profit of two pence on each, to be shared with the stall owner. The stall itself is a wooden bench and a table beside the road. The coffee is Nescafé.

Demo gets up before daybreak to be at the stall by 5 am, when the town has already come to life. He works the breakfast trade until 9 am and then takes a break until after lunch. Back again at 2 pm, he is on the stall till midnight — altogether a 14-hour working day.

For entertainment, Demo goes to the cinema sometimes when he has an evening off. He takes his work seriously and is not interested in trying to get rich quick by joining the diggers at one of the gold-rush sites near Dori. After all, he pointed out, the equipment is expensive and you also have to pay for the water for panning. Then, if in the end you don't find any gold, you are worse off than before.

GOLD AT ANY PRICE

Tens of thousands of the poor and hungry have been drawn across Burkina's desert fringe by the lure of gold.

On the way to Fété-Kolé there is scarcely a landmark from one horizon to the other — just bare, stony land with a scattering of dry shrubs and thorn trees. Occasionally we pass one or two people on foot, a few goats, and then, from out of nowhere, a splendid camel bearing two men attired in rich robes: the one in front wearing a fez-like hat gleaming with gold embroidery, the one behind carrying a shiny leather briefcase. They disappear, almost like a mirage, in the dust behind us.

Eventually the mounds of excavated ore around Fété-Kolé come into view. The settlement consists of makeshift shacks, built from a few pieces of wood and covered with mats woven from millet stalks. Living conditions are harsh. There is no sanitation. A flock of vultures, silhouetted against the sky, look from a distance like leaves on a dead tree.

Whole families come here to seek their fortune, or merely survival. The young men hack out the ore from the ground; the old ones, the women and the children sit on the ground pounding the stones to pieces, grinding them to dust and then panning for the magic metal.

The government has given the gold-diggers a free rein, on condition that they sell exclusively to the state. In fact, that condition is widely ignored. The diggers do provide the government with a revenue of £6 million a year, but the price they receive — £5 per gram — is well below the market rate in neighbouring countries. As a result, anything up to 80 per cent of the gold dug at these sites is smuggled abroad. This loss to the Burkina treasury is further compounded by the fact that the prospectors' crude techniques are able to extract less than half the actual gold content of the ore. Given that gold, on the official trade alone, has now overtaken cotton and livestock as the country's principal export, the lack of effective control and management of this key resource amounts to a serious economic haemorrhage.

The one fully industrial goldmine, at Poura, with reserves of 22 tons and possibly much more, is owned 60 per cent by the government and 40 per cent by foreign interests. But it has been accused of neo-colonial management practices, with the lion's share of pay and profits going to expatriates.

At Asakane, not far from Gorom-Gorom in the Oudalan, the conditions of the gold-diggers are if anything worse than at Fété-Kolé. There was no settlement at Asakane until 1985, when one family discovered gold by chance. Now, in the dry season, up to 25,000 people cram into the area and quick money has disrupted the social fabric with crime, drug-taking and prostitution. Some observers estimate that four out of every five prostitutes at Asakane carry the AIDS virus. The lack of sanitation has also encouraged epidemics of measles, malaria, meningitis, yellow fever and respiratory infections. With only two water pumps for the whole population, some prospectors have dug their own wells, but the contaminated water only spreads diarrhoeal diseases, cholera, typhoid and conjunctivitis.

Often excavating through solid rock, the Asakane miners dig holes 30 metres deep or more. Some days they may be lucky and find one or two grams, but more often they get nothing. Many take drugs to enable them to keep working round the clock; they even drug the donkeys which carry the ore. Squatting beside their huts, men with dust-whitened faces and the blank expression of zombies shake and shake their sieves. A bit further along the dirt road there are market stalls selling motorbikes, videos, radiocassettes and furniture. The contrasts are painful, and yet the mask-like faces seem to be saying: 'This may be hell, but at least there's some kind of hope here. Show us a better way to escape the bonds of our poverty.'

Panning for gold near Kalsaka, Yatenga province.
(Mark Edwards/Oxfam)

HOLDING UP HALF THE SKY

A woman's life in the Sahel is a more relentless struggle — against hunger, against sickness, against social inferiority, against natural disasters — than almost anywhere else on earth. When she is born in rural Burkina Faso, she can't expect to live much beyond 40. She has a 1-in-15 chance of going to school at all, and less than a one per cent chance of reaching secondary school. She starts work at an early age, gets married and will have an average of seven children. At least one of them will probably die in infancy. Her working hours are often twice as long as those of a man.

In his speech defining the political orientation of the revolution in 1983, Thomas Sankara proclaimed that women 'hold up the other half of the sky'. It was his commitment to emancipating them from the system of slavery which he said women had endured for thousands of years. Sankara denounced polygamy and the traditions of social and family organisation which reduced women to being 'beasts of burden', and he urged them to stand up for themselves against exploitative, feudal husbands.

Sadly, Sankara's rhetoric produced few practical reforms. When a National Women's Week presented him with a list of concrete ideas, including a family code with a minimum legal age for marriage and the outlawing of forced marriages, they went unheeded. Instead, Sankara launched fruitless campaigns against prostitution and female circumcision. Nevertheless, his impassioned appeals to Burkinabè women to assert their rights may have had a more lasting impact than any legislation in changing their image of themselves. Inspired by his oratory, women gained confidence in the value of their work and started to insist that their menfolk respect it. The results may be detected in the fact that many local women's groups have sprung up in recent times, perhaps to run a village mill or to organise a handicrafts co-operative.

A Lobi woman walking to market in Gaoua, near Bobo-Dioulasso.
(Jeremy Hartley/Oxfam)

Grinding millet for the evening meal, Noogo village, Yatenga province.
(Jeremy Hartley/Oxfam)

But while much of the daily toil is common to all women of the Sahel — tending crops, pounding grain, gathering wood and water, caring for the family — there is a marked difference between ethnic groups in their personal freedom and social status. Once married, for example, a Mossi woman has little economic or social independence; she is traditionally under the strict control of her husband, who considers this essential to ensure her fidelity. Besides working in his fields, it is her responsibility to feed and clothe the children.

By contrast, among the Lobi people in the south west of the country, women have a large measure of independence and freedom of movement. Theirs is a matrilinear culture, tracing the family line through mother rather than father — something which is common in the region among people from the forest zones. Not only do Lobi children take their mother's family name and belong to her clan, but a husband cannot claim exclusive rights to fathering his wife's children. Lobi women are active in trade and would never think of telling their husbands how much they earn. And while he is required to provide his wife with food, she has no obligation to serve him meals.

In society at large, equality for women is coming nearer, but slowly. It conflicts with deeply-rooted social traditions, which tend to inhibit change. Change, nevertheless, is occurring; the basic question is how fast the social fabric can absorb it without being torn apart.

THE GRIOT'S THIRD WIFE

This is the brief history of a girl called Batuma, who lives in Ouagadougou.

At a young age, Batuma was given in marriage to a *griot* (a traditional story-teller), who already had two wives. She now has three small children. Batuma does not know how old she is and has never gone to school.

Her husband's income is irregular, so she and her co-wives have to support themselves and their children. Batuma earns a little money by frying doughnuts and yams for sale on the street. She also takes on extra chores such as washing bedclothes for a hotel in the neighbourhood.

Her home consists of two small rooms in a yard, in a district where the buildings are under threat of demolition. She does not have a kitchen, so she prepares food under a tree in the yard, buying firewood daily for the purpose. Sometimes she can manage only one meal a day; otherwise, if she has been able to save some coal, she will heat up leftovers in the evening. Occasionally she is given a little coal by a neighbour who brews dôlo.

Batuma cannot afford to vary her children's diet. Mostly she cooks tô with sauce made from okra and leaves. She has a few hens, but they seem to be suffering from some sickness and she is not sure they will survive. If they die, she says, she will use them to make stew.

Titao village, Yatenga province: Mrs Aguierra Ouédraogo winnowing millet.
(Jeremy Hartley/Oxfam)

WISHING FOR HEALTH AND POWER

'When we go to bed, our prayer is to wake up healthy, and on waking, to have enough to eat.'

It is Mrs Aguierra Ouédraogo speaking. She is president of the Women's Group in the village of Titao, in northern Yatenga Province. The Group has convened a special meeting for our visit and laid out an impressive display of the produce they sell: dried fish and onions, tomato powder, sesame biscuits, and a variety of cakes.

What would the women of Titao most wish for, to improve their lives? — 'My wish would be to have a bit of power to change things, to help other members of my family and people who are ill or handicapped.'

Who has that power? — 'Wende.' (God)

But in this world? — 'In this world it's men who have the power, and it's right that they do, because they have the experience and they travel a lot. If we could do the same, that would be the ideal — to go to the big towns, to meetings and so on. But for the time being we go no further than this market.'

Do you think that can change? — 'We can reach the ideal if men give us the freedom. Meanwhile, we can go some way towards it in meetings like this, because unity is strength.'

The women of Titao split off from the overall Village Group when they realised they were never free if they worked with the men, who took all the decisions. They formed sub-groups and went to each other's houses to share work, then had the idea of hiring out their labour as a group. Profits are held by the Group, which then makes grants to members when they have special needs. To strengthen their activities, the Women's Group sought help from Oxfam, which is now supporting their work.

Women pounding karité nuts to make shea nut butter, Noogo village, Yatenga province.
(Jeremy Hartley/Oxfam)

The Group meets twice a month. It now has 90 members and more want to join. Even the men are satisfied, they say, partly because there are some things which they recognise women can do better, and also because they are earning money and their husbands have less need to support them.

But Mrs Ouédraogo's nightly prayer for health reflects a harsh reality. In the poverty of these dryland settlements, sickness is the dreaded spectre at everyone's door. At any given time, only 40 of the Women's Group's 90 members are healthy enough to work, and probably half of those will be pregnant. Family planning, then? Well, that was something that had been brought by whites. They were not convinced: afraid it could have side effects. Anyway, someone joked, things had been so hard this year the men wouldn't have any strength left for reproductive activities. That got a good laugh all round.

WORDS DON'T COME EASY ...

Undoubtedly, Burkina Faso's richest resource is its people. According to the World Bank, Burkina stands out in the region for the quality of its men and women, who, it says, are well reputed for their diligence, resourcefulness and adaptability. But long-term prosperity, the Bank adds, will depend on their capacity to adopt new techniques, new tools, new products.

That is the narrow economic view. Advancement will also depend, more fundamentally, on their ability to participate in the *process* of development, to understand what is going on, and to contribute to the decisions that affect their lives. To comprehend the scale of the challenge facing their government, it is enough to know that five out of six Burkinabès could not read a word on this page, even if it were written in their own language. Reading, writing and a basic education are what, more than anything, separate Burkina's privileged classes from their seven-and-a-half million illiterate compatriots.

The government has made sustained efforts to improve literacy rates. In the 13 years up to 1988, some 340,000 people were given training, but in the early years many soon forgot what they had learned. Today, many students joining the 'Operation Alpha' literacy campaign are more keenly motivated, but there is still a serious lack of printed material in their own language to sustain new readers. There is only one occasional magazine in the most widely spoken national language, Mooré, and in fact illiteracy is growing rather than declining, as a result of population growth. Among women, who are the most underprivileged, the literacy rate in rural areas is as low as two per cent.

In terms of formal education, Burkina faces a huge uphill task. Only slightly more than a quarter of the country's children are able to find school places — one of the lowest enrolment rates in Africa. The current target is to raise enrolment to 40 per cent by 1996.

In fact, great strides have been made since the revolution. In five years, more than 1,000 schools were built by townspeople and villagers under the programme of popular mobilisation, raising the primary school intake by 150,000, and more than doubling the numbers in secondary schools. But at the present rate of education spending, it will still be more than a century before all children can find a school place.

Despite a national school-building campaign since the revolution, places are available for fewer than half the children of Burkina.
(Mark Edwards/Oxfam)

A LIMITED RIGHT TO KNOW

There has been only one brand of public information available until now in Burkina: the government's own. Attempts to establish independent media outlets were abruptly stamped on. The government-controlled, French-language *Sidwaya* is the sole daily newspaper, with a circulation of about 4,000 copies. Its title means 'Here's The Truth', but the Burkinabès, like the British, enjoy playing with words. Some subversive wits renamed it *Zirwaya* — 'Here Are The Lies'.

Outsiders often criticise African governments for preventing a free flow of information to their people. And at one level, such criticism is presumptuous, when the countries concerned have only 30 years of nationhood behind them and a largely illiterate population. Many Northern governments differ only in the sophistication with which they suppress things they don't want the people to know.

At another level, however, many African commentators agree that the people's lack of access to independent information stifles their energies and the contribution they could make to national development. Censorship, by protecting those in power, also protects corruption and incompetence, as well as presenting a distorted mirror of reality.

In Burkina there are signs of change: in mid-1990 a new Information Code became law, legalising public debate in the information media. A private radio station, which had been banned a year earlier for refusing to broadcast official communiqués, was planning to reopen.

Apart from *Sidwaya*, there is one newspaper in the main national language, Mooré, which appears a few times a year. But the print media reach only one person in 5,000, whereas almost every family by now has a transistor radio. The national radio service broadcasts 100 hours a week, but more than half of its output is in French — understood by only a small proportion of the population — while 16 national languages get an average of no more than three hours each. Community groups are now at least getting better access to the airwaves of the Rural Radio Service, which broadcasts village debates, music and entertainment, and programmes for women. Thursday is the day for rural radio broadcasts in Burkina, and, in the words of one of its presenters, Seydou Drame, 'The farmer gets on his bicycle and rides off to his field with a hoe, some water, and his radio, to keep him company while he works. It's up to us to keep him interested, because if he gets bored he can turn to Radio Mali, Radio Benin, or Africa 1. By giving people access to the airwaves themselves, we're discovering the need for a peasant-to-peasant dialogue.' The first two of six local radio stations are also in operation, funded by their local communities and with technical support but no finance from central government.

Goumba village, Yatenga province: listening to the radio while making rope from the threads of nylon sacks.
(Jeremy Hartley/Oxfam)

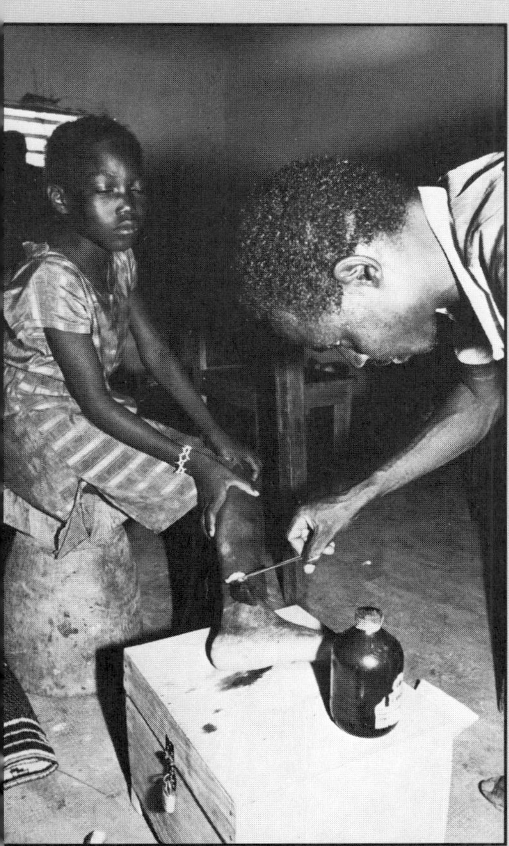

Primary health post, Noogo village, Yatenga province.
(Jeremy Hartley/Oxfam)

BULLETS BEFORE BANDAGES

An old man in the village is sick. He tries to ignore the pain, knowing he cannot afford the cost of modern treatment, and hoping the ailment will cure itself. Instead it gets worse, so he goes to seek out the traditional doctor in the village, whose herbal remedies have sometimes worked in the past. This time they don't, and he is by now very ill. As a last resort he appeals to members of his family for help to get to the nearest doctor or health centre, perhaps 50 kilometres away. But it's been a bad season, many others have been sick and his relatives have no help left to give. The old man returns to his hut; there is nothing more to do. He lies down, maybe to die.

Stories such as this are an everyday reality in rural Burkina. In a country of 7,200 villages there are only 154 dispensaries and 20 maternity units; one doctor for every 31,000 people, one pharmacist for every 85,000. Most health care is still located in the cities, even though in 1985 the Sankara government launched a big campaign to shift resources to the rural areas.

The government's most spectacular success was the massive operation 'Vaccination Commando' in which nearly three million children were vaccinated against measles, meningitis and yellow fever. The first two of these, together with malaria and diarrhoeal diseases, are the principal killers in a country where the infant mortality rate is 134 per thousand. But another commando-style health operation — to establish a primary health care post (PSP) in every village of the country — soon began to fall apart after an initial fever of activity. One voluntary agency which had hoped to support the PSP programme attributed its failure to a number of causes: lack of preparation, poor choice of village health agents, who were often illiterate, and lack of supervision. In addition, supplies of simple equipment and medicines promised to the PSPs often didn't arrive. Many of the posts have since closed.

Inept planning may deserve its share of blame, but the bare fact is that health care has not been given the priority it needs in government budgeting to reach the majority of people with even minimal services. One example: only five per cent of the rural population have access to a toilet, and only one person in three has a source of clean drinking water. Use of stagnant or contaminated water is the cause of many illnesses.

But while the country's population has been growing rapidly, expenditure on health has slumped from 10 per cent of the national budget in the mid-1970s to 6.2 per cent in 1987. Over approximately the same period, military spending has soared from 11.5 to 19 per cent of the national budget. The priorities of the Revolution are statistically clear: bullets before bandages. For its part, the World Bank is encouraging the government to allocate more resources to the health sector. Yet in its two volumes of recommendations for restructuring the Burkina economy, the Bank has not one word to say about possible economies in military spending, which devours one-fifth of all the money in the government's coffers. Some things, evidently, are still sacrosanct.

THE PRESSURE OF NUMBERS

Burkina Faso is a young country, not only in the political sense but especially in the youth of its people. At the start of the 1990s, almost half of the population are under the age of 15. With a progressive reduction in infant mortality rates over the past two decades, and with so many young people now approaching child-bearing age, population policy will be critical if they are to have any kind of sustainable future.

Since 1985, the government has promoted family planning as an integral part of maternal and child health care. Laws forbidding the advertising of contraceptives were abolished in 1986, and family planning policy in general is considered more progressive than in most other African countries. Resistance to family planning is said to come largely from men, fearing the freedom it might give their womenfolk; but in the villages quite a lot of older men — their wives perhaps past child-bearing age — now say it's the only way they can see of reducing pressures on the land caused by the ever-growing number of mouths to feed. One of the problems, pointed out by older people of both sexes, is that the younger generation no longer observes the traditional rule of restraint whereby husbands were supposed to ensure at least three years' spacing between their wives' children. Taboos such as this have lost their force as the old patterns of family and tribal authority disintegrate. It is one small example of how the outside world, with its seductive messages of modernisation, has disrupted the delicate balances of forces on which survival here depends.

In the colonial period and right up to independence, Burkina was seen by the French administration as an ideal reservoir of labour for their plantations, construction sites and other enterprises in the neighbouring colony of Ivory Coast. For a time, a system of forced labour was even introduced to ensure a sufficient supply of manpower. By now, it is estimated, nearly one-third of the Ivory Coast's population is of Burkinabè origin. There was also a steady migration of young men to the Gold Coast (now Ghana) in search of money to pay the bride price or buy land back home.

Still today, about three-quarters of a million Burkinabès are working abroad at any one time, though numbers have been declining as the coastal states themselves feel the pinch of hard times. The money that the migrants send home, currently totalling £56 million a year, represents a sizeable chunk of the nation's income. It also gives the returning émigrés — mostly younger men — an importance in their village which they could not have had in former times, when the traditional authority of the elders held sway.

With four out of every ten of the adult male population now working abroad, the women left at home obviously have to carry extra burdens. They are responsible for looking after their husbands' land and livestock, without ever having the right to acquire land for their own security.

In recent years an international campaign to eradicate river blindness in Burkina and the surrounding region has opened up new fertile lands in the south west of the country for migrants from the drought-stricken Sahel. Yet as these migratory flows continue and shift, the most acute pressure in the coming generation seems certain to be on the towns and cities. Twenty years ago the capital, Ouagadougou, was a modest mudbrick town of 100,000 souls. At the start of the 1990s it is home to half a million, and in a mere 20 years more it is expected to reach 1,550,000.

Family planning sign in Gaoua, near Bobo-Dioulasso.
(Jeremy Hartley/Oxfam)

CONCRETE REPLACES MUD — BUT WHO CAN AFFORD IT?

More than half the urban areas of Burkina consist of spontaneous, unplanned settlements where people have simply moved in and built their own houses or shacks on open land. They are do-it-yourself shanty towns with little in the way of sanitation or other services. And on top of the pressures created by the doubling of Ouagadougou's population in the past ten years, in the Sahel as a whole the number of people living in towns is expected to quadruple by the year 2010.

To cope with acute housing needs in the capital, the government in 1984 initiated a major building programme, aiming to redevelop one section of the city for each year of the revolution. 'Homes for the People' was the slogan. But the choice of costly building techniques meant that average rentals in Third Year City had to be set at £70 a month, far beyond the reach of the average Burkinabè.

A more promising approach is the sites-and-services scheme designed to permit planned development for the whole of Ouagadougou. Under this plan, parcels of land — 300 or 400 square metres — are allocated in the squatter settlements, as far as possible to their existing occupants. In return for a fee of £50 and an undertaking to upgrade their homes, they get a residency permit and a promise of basic services. By the end of 1987, some 60,000 parcels had been allocated, but at a high cost to the people. The new boundaries seldom coincided with their old ones, so many had to rebuild: their savings were wiped out and they had to start again. Many of the poorest, and those with no existing buildings on their land, were forced out altogether.

Meanwhile, a frenzy of construction activity is rapidly transforming the centre of Ouagadougou, with its low mudbrick buildings and wide avenues, into a mini-metropolis of concrete and glass. For many international aid agencies with their regional headquarters here, Ouaga since the drought of the 1970s has been the unofficial capital of the Sahel, and it seems determined to consolidate that status. More than £60 million has been invested in the current building boom, two-thirds of it by the government for new offices and housing. The splendid new central market, Rood Woko, completed in 1988, alone cost £10 million.

The nagging question, however, is whether such an undeveloped agricultural country can really afford all this expensive centralised infrastructure. It's true that until recently Burkina has indulged less in extravagant construction projects than many other African countries — and that a sizeable chunk of current building investment is said to come from individual Burkinabès who have been accumulating funds in Ivory Coast. Nevertheless, the extent of government financing of the building boom begins to look disproportionate when only a small proportion of foreign aid, and less than five per cent of the government's own budget, is devoted to the agriculture on which four-fifths of its people depend.

A common sight in Ouagadougou's commercial zone.

(Jeremy Hartley/Oxfam)

POWER FOR THE PEOPLE IS STILL FIREWOOD

With electricity a luxury confined to the few major towns, the average Burkinabè household depends on firewood for 90 per cent of its energy needs — for cooking, for heating bath water, for brewing dôlo beer and for other income-earning activities such as textile-dyeing. Which means that each adult needs about a kilo of wood — the equivalent of one small log — every day. For the country as a whole, therefore, four million logs a day: a measure of the basic human needs which have to be confronted in the struggle against deforestation.

Since the government introduced controls on wood-cutting, people in some areas have been increasingly forced to burn millet straw, other crop residues and sometimes cow dung — resources which could otherwise be used to help regenerate their soil. So measures to save the trees may have the effect of impoverishing the earth: sometimes it seems there is a Catch-22 in every attempt to rationalise the development process.

At the beginning of the 1980s, after the second major leap in world oil prices, Burkina found that nearly three-quarters of all its export earnings were being eaten up by energy imports. When Sankara came to power, it was decided to construct a hydro-electric dam, which, it was reckoned, would meet 20-30 per cent of the nation's power requirements and save over £4 million on its annual fuel bill. The Kompienga dam, on the southern border with Ghana, cost £73 million and was completed in 1988, on time and within budget. Apart from the electricity output, its artificial lake is designed to irrigate 2,000 hectares for agriculture. The planners say it could also produce 1,500 tons of fish a year.

Now work has begun on a second and even more ambitious hydro-electric scheme — the Bagré dam — which, in a sparsely populated area of Boulgou province, aims ultimately to irrigate 30,000 hectares and provide settlements with a livelihood for 120,000 people. The authorities say they intend to involve the new peasant-settlers in developing the project, building 23 small villages in the first phase up to 1993. According to the technical director, each village will house members of one ethnic group and will have control over its own land. Settlers will farm in the traditional way to meet their own food needs, and use the irrigated land to grow rice for sale.

There are plans for an even bigger dam on the Mouhoun River on the border with Ghana, which would have an output equal to Kompienga and Bagré combined. The price-tag is £200 million, but Noumbiel would make the country virtually self-sufficient in energy at the beginning of the next century — that is, provided the water supply from rainfall does not decline. In fact, the predicted general impact of global warming is a movement of climatic zones from the equator towards the poles, and if that applies here, it could improve the prospects for hydro power.

There are, however, other questions about the viability and the environmental impact of large dam projects. Fisheries in the dams of Lake Volta, Ghana, and Lake Kariba, Zambia, started off with impressive catches, but later declined rapidly as lake vegetation rotted away and fish stocks fell. Elsewhere, problems of salinity and waterlogging on irrigated land have drastically reduced agricultural productivity, while large dams have proved good breeding grounds for the black fly which carries the worm causing river blindness. The problems likely to arise with Burkina's hydro-power programme are still incubating.

Buying charcoal from the government-controlled store in Ouagadougou. One sack costs £1.30. The wood comes from Kompienga, on the Togo border; only licensed traders can sell it.
(Jeremy Hartley/Oxfam)

GETTING ABOUT

For people in the countryside, a donkey cart or a push-bike is the main means of transport. With pot-holed tracks seldom repaired and made worse in the rainy season, even getting to the nearest town — for medical care or to take produce to market — can be an arduous undertaking. Between towns there are bush taxis — rickety wagons squashing in passengers and their belongings like sardines — or sometimes regular bus services. Burkina has 13,000 km of roads, of which a little more than one-tenth are surfaced; the rest are dirt tracks of varying quality.

In the towns, the moped is undisputed king of the roads. Mopeds or scooters are affordable now for many with regular city jobs, who can buy petrol by the bottle from little roadside stalls. When the traffic lights turn green in Ouagadougou, the moped battalions surge across the intersections with a buzzing crescendo like a swarm of bees.

For a landlocked country shut in by six foreign states around its borders, the development of regional transport links is vital if Burkina is to reduce its isolation and its import/export costs. In fact, over the past two decades the country has built up a considerable transport infrastructure and has become a hub for much of the region's traffic. Much of it, though, is in a bad state of disrepair, and the cost of maintenance rises year by year.

The French planned a railway line from the port of Abidjan which would cross Burkina and continue eastwards to Niamey, the capital of Niger. The company to run it was called the Régie Abidjan-Niger (RAN), but the line never got further than Ouagadougou. Inherited jointly by the governments of Burkina and the Ivory Coast, RAN played an important role in Burkina's foreign trade and economic development. In recent times, however, the service has piled up huge debts and much traffic has switched to the roads. Having now been split into two separate national companies, the service is in bad shape, leading the World Bank to observe that 'radical measures urgently need to be taken to prevent the operational and financial collapse of the railway'.

Air Burkina, the national airline, has two planes providing services to neighbouring countries. It also manages the presidential Boeing 727, alleged by some to be an extravagance but which, it is said, spends most of its time on commercial lease. The first customer to rent it was pop star Michael Jackson.

Ouagadougou - where the moped reigns supreme.
(Jeremy Hartley/Oxfam)

IS ALL THIS AID DOING ANY GOOD?

A lot of people are sceptical about the benefits of foreign aid, in Burkina itself as well as outside. Official aid from foreign governments and international agencies effectively doubles the national budget of the government: in 1988 it topped US$300 million, and there are currently 240 big aid projects in progress around the country, each with a budget of £200,000 or more. Burkina has eleven principal donors, including UN agencies, the European Community, the African Development Bank, and the governments of France, the United States, Canada, Germany and the Netherlands. After them come a string of 24 more international and government aid agencies.

In 1988 alone, Burkina had to cope with more than 700 visiting missions from the aid donors: experts wanting to discuss the government's plans, to evaluate projects in progress, to look at possible new ones, and then to evaluate some more. Seven hundred whirlwind tours by more or less knowledgeable foreigners, any one of whose opinions could have an important influence on some chunk of the country's future. Yet driving through the country, and especially in the poorest and neediest northern provinces, one is hard pressed to find evidence that the grand schemes of the past 30 years have made any real difference to people's lives.

How can this be? The hundreds of millions of francs, dollars and deutschmarks given or loaned to Burkina and other countries of the Sahel in the last three decades — have they really all been wasted? For better or worse, the answers are not so simple, but it is perhaps important to try to identify some of the factors responsible for what many admit is a fairly dismal record.

Some of the recurrent failings of official aid are well illustrated by a five-year, 29-million dollar project which was launched in the eastern region of Burkina in 1982. It aimed to increase food crop production and farmers' incomes, and to strengthen rural organisation. Financed by the International Fund for Agricultural Development, the governments of France and the United States, and the UN Development Programme, it was designed to benefit 40,000 of the poorest people in the country.

By the end of 1987, when the project was supposed to wind up, very little had been achieved. It had 'reached' more than the 8,000 farmers originally planned, but basically they weren't much interested. Fewer than 10 per cent of them had received the credits they were supposed to get to buy agricultural inputs, equipment and farm animals. Anti-erosion works covered less than half the original target area, none of the four planned

A solar-powered cooker, designed and made in Europe - without much reference to local needs: village women cook in the evenings, not at mid-day (when most heat is produced); and the pot is too small for a family meal.
(Maggie Murray/Format)

In the background: a solar-powered pump, paid for by the European Community. It fails to supply enough water, so the traditional well in the foreground, which it was meant to replace, is still in use.
(Maggie Murray/Format)

'Even if the rich man dances badly, one says he dances well.' — Mossi proverb

dispensaries had been built, only 10 of 100 wells had been dug, and only one per cent of the funds earmarked for village enterprises had been allocated. The project was supposed to rehabilitate 1,000 hectares of land for rice production; it managed 36 hectares, which were promptly wiped out by the first flood. An evaluation report in February 1987 observed laconically: 'Project impact at this point is poor.'

Lessons from this experience can be learnt: first, the project suffered from *the techno-fix syndrome*, which occurs when the experts reckon that they are dealing with purely technical problems and that their job — what they've been paid for — is to produce the purest technical solutions. How else to explain that a project can go on misfiring for five years, at enormous cost, without anyone blowing the whistle? It is not altogether the experts' fault, but sadly, theories and sand do not mix well. *Ignorance of place and people* was the second problem: the experts didn't know the farmers or their needs, otherwise they wouldn't have been urging them to grow crops they couldn't sell. Only very late in the day did the project realise there were no adequate market outlets.

The third problem was *tunnel vision*. Projects are still too often designed in a vacuum, far from the real-life pressures and concerns of the people for whom they are intended. The planners isolate one problem for treatment, but things go wrong when the project finds that people have other ideas and priorities, and will not conform with its single-track plan.

Other official aid projects suffer from *self-interest* on the part of the donors, which means that projects are selected which best suit their commercial or other interests, rather than those which might be most use to the recipients. Projects, for example, which give them an excuse to provide their own expensive equipment, vehicles, fertilisers, and so on. Or projects from which they can cream the benefit, such as the promotion of export crops. Consequently, only a tiny fraction of official aid for the Sahel goes to develop the kind of rainfed agriculture on which 80 per cent of the people depend, and less than two per cent is given for reforestation and environmental projects.

Finally, a tendency which is sometimes called *clientelism* dictates that donors, in return for the latitude they are given in choosing projects, do not choose any that the host government would object to. Thus aid tends to reinforce the interests of governments, rather than the interests of the people.

But, as Jacques Giri, an experienced French commentator on the Sahel, has pointed out, the fundamental flaw in the whole process of official aid is that it has sought to provide the capital necessary to stimulate and sustain economic growth — as if the economy was something which could be treated separately from the complex web of cultural and social structures and relationships which go to make up any society. Maybe, he says, the assumption was that economic growth would permeate and promote change at all levels. But it hasn't worked, because Sahelian societies are not like that. The fragility of their physical environment belies a metaphysical strength and resilience which up till now has confounded all the one-dimensional strategies which the world has tried to foist upon them.

Food aid brings dubious benefits: it tends to drive down local prices and reduce farmers' incentives to grow their own produce.

(Mark Edwards/Oxfam)

WHO IS HELPING WHOM?

Since the drought of the 1970s, non-governmental organisations (NGOs) have taken a front-line role in helping and working with the peasants of Burkina. The Northern NGOs, in particular, are a many-flavoured assortment of non-profit-making development agencies and church groups from Europe and North America. Some are highly professional, with many years' experience in the region; others are primarily concerned with placing volunteers to work in local communities, and others again come armed with bread and Bibles.

But people-to-people help from overseas is not now exclusively from the rich North. In one of the remotest Sahelian villages, there is the saffron-robed resident field worker of an Indian NGO, helping to develop community initiatives. Some of the villagers, he told us, are now keenly learning yoga.

As the big aid-giving countries have become more conscious of the thin results achieved by government-to-government aid, they have channelled an increasing share through their NGOs. Consequently, in many countries like Burkina, the NGOs have become the biggest fish in the pond. They are often the only ones to have the rugged, off-road vehicles necessary for getting out to the villages, and the only ones who can afford the petrol to go where they will. Government staff and extension workers have no such freedom of movement.

The Canadian Save the Children Fund has calculated that aid to Burkina Faso from all NGOs in 1986 amounted to £26 million. Though a lot higher than a United Nations estimate, if the Canadian SCF reckoning is correct, it would mean that NGOs are contributing something equivalent to 18 per cent of Burkina's national budget.

By the mid-80s there were more than 70 different foreign NGOs operating in the country. One result has been the emergence of a new breed of indigenous NGOs. The foreign agencies needed partners through whom to implement their projects, so in some cases they were instrumental in creating local organisations for the purpose; in others, it was former government officials or people educated abroad who recognised a bandwagon when they saw one and quickly climbed aboard, setting up their own associations.

Some of the best of the Burkina NGOs today, however, are exceptions to this trend. Catholic missionary orders with long experience in the country have given rise to two Burkina-based development training organisations with a widely-respected track record. CESAO — the West African Centre for Economic and Social Studies — was founded by the White Fathers in 1960. Based in Bobo Dioulasso, CESAO has evolved a programme of training and support for rural organisations which is highly regarded by government and voluntary organisations alike.

Working on similar lines is the *Groupe de Recherche et d'Appui pour l'Autopromotion Paysanne* (GRAAP), established by the Dominican order and likewise based in Bobo Dioulasso. And then there is the Federation of the *Groupements Naam*, which is not only an autonomous national movement but has also an authentic social base, with 200,000 peasants linked to it.

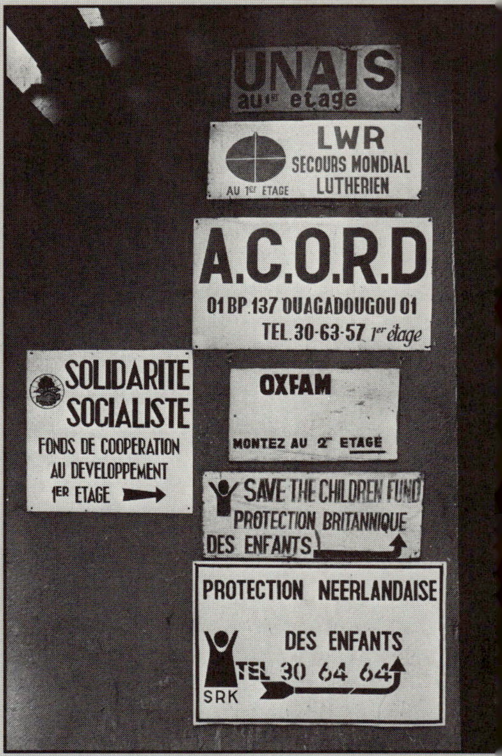

A few of the 70 foreign development agencies based in Ouagadougou share an office block with Oxfam.
(Jeremy Hartley/Oxfam)

xfam worker Daouda Ouédraogo elping children to plant acacia eedlings along a diguette line in oumba village, Yatenga province. mall-scale community-based developent work is the key to Oxfam's rogramme in Burkina.
eremy Hartley/Oxfam)

Another Burkinabè NGO within the Catholic community is a development studies centre, the *Bureau d'Etudes et de Liaison*. BEL sees the services of NGOs being more in demand than ever, because government support to the rural areas has declined. But BEL believes that the work of NGOs needs to develop a stronger economic focus. So far, it is argued, projects have concentrated on social needs; they should now give greater emphasis to helping people become productive through income-generating initiatives, and training them so they can be more independent.

This, indeed, underlines a problem faced by many indigenous Sahelian NGOs themselves. Their Northern partners will provide the funding for projects, but are seldom prepared to help with the training or institutional support needed if they are to become effective and fully-fledged development agencies. In some other countries, African NGOs are now — with justice — demanding such support as a condition for accepting project work. It ought soon to happen here, too.

FUTURE CONDITIONAL

Thinking about the future is first a consequence and then a cause of change. For the people of Burkina Faso, seeing unprecedented change all around them — encouraging, tantalising, threatening — the future is something they will have to struggle to control for themselves. What can they hope to make of it?

The first certainty is that the people of Burkina will have not one but many futures. One for the peasants, another for the town-dwellers; one for the arid north, another for the more fertile south; one for the literate, another for the rest; one for the rich, another for the poor. And all of them will reflect the cruel contradictions which beset this landlocked fragment of West Africa: the contradiction that civil society is beginning to find a new dynamism just as it faces a crisis of drastically diminishing options; the contradiction that steps to increase the country's self-sufficiency in one domain plunge it deeper into dependency of some other kind. There are other paradoxes, too — not least that of the country's 'revolutionary capitalist' leadership — and how they resolve themselves will determine the futures available for the people.

Global warming may bring more or less drought in the next 25 years. We just don't know. The hundreds of self-help land-reclamation schemes which at best might conceivably herald a renaissance of the Sahel could equally be wiped out by increasingly erratic weather forcing the abandonment of habitation in the arid zone.

As for what is controllable, many economists and aid planners assert that Burkina and other countries of the Sahel will need even larger doses of foreign assistance over the next 20 years. They maintain that substantial increases in aid and investment will be needed, just to keep these countries alive and to give them some chance of making their economies viable. But this kind of medicine, others argue, risks being worse than the disease. It should be decreased, they say, not stepped up, because conventional forms of government-to-government aid tend to lead resource-poor countries like Burkina into ever greater debt and dependency. Unless an entirely new structure can be devised to supervise resource transfers from North to South (and there is no sign of it at present), Burkina could in due course find itself in the same trap as many Third World countries today — having to pay out substantially more each year to Northern creditors than they receive in aid.

The first of these analyses is the one most likely to prevail, because it suits the vested interests of both donor and recipient countries. The revolution under Sankara tried to go the other way — the route of self-reliance — but Compaoré has decided to play the game by World Bank rules. One of the main fears of African governments now is that the recent dramatic developments in eastern Europe will prompt aid-giving western countries to cut their losses in Africa and concentrate on the new opportunities for investment there.

So the future is conditional on many crucial *ifs*. It is a future fraught with peril, even if that is nothing new for people who have survived half a lifetime of drought and famines. Some will succumb, but one way or another the spirit and will of the people of Burkina will endure, and one is left with the memory of that Yatenga village and its peasant leader, Guiro Mahama, declaring defiantly: *'Now we are dynamic and determined to go ahead. You can't help a man who is asleep, but we are awake, standing up and determined to progress.'*

A girl of the Bella tribe in Gorom-Gorom, Oudalan province.
(Jeremy Hartley/Oxfam)

FACTS AND FIGURES

Area:	274,000 sq km (slightly bigger than the United Kingdom)
Population:	8.8 million (1989 estimate)
Population growth rate:	2.7 per cent per annum
Main ethnic groups:	Mossi, Peul, Lobi, Mandé, Bobo, Gourounsi, Gourmantché, Sénoufou
Life expectancy:	48 years
Climate:	Three climatic zones: the Sahelian (north), maximum annual rainfall 300 mm; Sudano-Sahelian (central), max. rainfall 300-600 mm; Sudano-Guinean (south/south west), rainfall 600-1200 mm.
Religion:	Traditional animist 60 per cent, Moslem 30 per cent, Christian 10 per cent (all approximate)
Languages:	Official language: French. Main national languages: Mooré, Dioula, Fulfuldé
Capital:	Ouagadougou (pop. 500,000). Other towns: Bobo Dioulasso (250,000), Koudougou (54,000), Ouahigouya (40,000)
Currency:	Franc CFA = 100 centimes (under a fixed exchange rate, 50 FCFA = 1 French franc)
National budget:	FCFA 100 billion (£200 million) (1988 est.)
Average income:	£135 p.a. per capita
Exports:	Gold, raw cotton, livestock, shea nuts, hides and skins, sesame seeds
Foreign debt:	£480 million (at 1 January 1988). Debt service as a percentage of export earnings, 1987: 12.7 per cent (due), 7.8 per cent (paid)

Preparing the evening meal in Titao village: the leaves of the baobab tree will go in the sauce which flavours the tô.
(Jeremy Hartley/Oxfam)

(Jeremy Hartley/Oxfam)

(Mark Edwards/Oxfam)

DATES AND EVENTS

1100-1400	An early branch of the Mossi people arises north of the River Niger and captures Timbuktu (1337) and other lands, before being finally defeated by Moslem forces of the Songhai empire.
Late 1400s	Naaba Oubri founds the Kingdom of Ouagadougou, marking the beginning of the Mossi empire.
Mid-1500s	Kingdom of Yatenga founded by a nephew of Naaba Oubri. The Kingdom of Ouagadougou, under one of his sons, is strengthened with a surrounding ring of principalities. The Mossi empire is consolidated over the next 350 years until the French colonial occupation.
1740s	Severe drought
1830s	Great famine called Zogoré provokes mass migration southwards from Yatenga.
1896	French troops march into Ouagadougou. Naaba Koutou, called Wobgo ('the Elephant Emperor'), escapes to exile. All the territory of present-day Burkina becomes part of French West Africa.
1913	Severe drought causes the 'Famine of Naaba Koabga'.
1914-18	World War I: conscripts from present-day Burkina and other French territories are sent to fight in the trenches.
1919	France divides its West African territories into two colonies: Upper Volta and French Sudan.
1932	Upper Volta is erased from the map when France divides the territory between French Sudan and its other colonies of Niger and the Ivory Coast.
1934	Railway from Abidjan reaches Bobo Dioulasso; the French introduce a system of forced labour to obtain workers from Upper Volta for plantations in Ivory Coast.
1940s	Six years of drought during the decade: 'Famine of Piiss'Wai'.
1945	The Voltaic Union, supported by the Mogho Naaba, campaigns for restoration of Upper Volta.
1947	Reunification of the colony of Upper Volta.
1950s	Political parties are formed, and campaign for independence.

1960	5 August: Upper Volta becomes an independent state, with Maurice Yameogo the first President of the Republic.
1966	Army coup led by Col. S. Lamizana overthrows First Republic.
1968	Start of long drought.
1970	Lamizana hands over power to a civil regime (under his presidency): the Second Republic.
1972/73	Famine crisis with deepening drought; 100,000 people believed to have died in the Sahel, and millions of cattle and sheep.
1974	Army coup dissolves the Assembly; Lamizana remains President.
Dec 74-Jan 75	First border war between Upper Volta and Mali.
1977	A new Constitution is promulgated, heralding a return to democracy: the Third Republic.
1980	Coup d'état by Col. Saye Zerbo; downfall of Third Republic. Constitution suspended.
1981	Return of drought after respite in late 1970s.
1982	Zerbo overthrown by military coup which installs Jean-Baptiste Ouédraogo as President, heading Council for the Salvation of the People (CSP).
1982/83	Drought becomes acute: driest years this century.
1983	10 January: CSP designates Captain Thomas Sankara as Prime Minister. 17 May: CSP leadership arrests Sankara, his comrades-in-arms Lingani and Zongo, and others. 27 May: Sankara freed after mass demonstrations in his support. 4 August: Ouédraogo regime overthrown; National Council of the Revolution (CNR) takes power, with Sankara as President and Blaise Compaoré, Lingani and Zongo making up the four 'historic leaders' of the Revolution.
1985	Burkina bombed by Malian aircraft. Five-day war: 100 Burkinabès and Malians killed. Ceasefire signed 29 December.
1987	15 October: Sankara assassinated, along with 12 aides. Popular Front led by Blaise Compaoré dissolves CNR and calls for popular support. Thousands parade in mourning past Sankara's makeshift grave.
1989	Two remaining 'historic leaders' of the revolution, Lingani and Zongo, summarily executed for allegedly plotting a coup.

Touareg man, Djibo cattle market.
(Jeremy Hartley/Oxfam)

Peul, Touareg, and Mossi traders gather in a cattle market at Djibo, Soum province.
(Jeremy Hartley/Oxfam)

SOURCES AND FURTHER READING

Cross, Nigel (1990), *The Sahel: The People's Right to Development*, London: Minority Rights Group

Grainger, Alan (1990), *The Threatening Desert*, London: Earthscan

Harrison, Paul (1987), *The Greening of Africa*, London: Paladin

Jansson, Eva (1988), *Women, Environment and Energy-saving Stoves:A Report from Burkina Faso*, Stockholm: Development Studies Unit, University of Stockholm

Oral History Project Report: Burkina Faso (1990), London: SOS Sahel (UK)

The Sahel Facing The Future (1988), Paris: OECD

Thomas Sankara Speaks: The Burkina Faso Revolution 1983-87 (1988), New York: Pathfinder Press

Timberlake, Lloyd (1985), *Africa in Crisis*, London: Earthscan

World Bank (89), *Burkina Faso Economic Memorandum, Vols I and II*, Washington: World Bank

Andriamirado, Sennen (1989), *Il s'appelait Sankara*, Paris: Jeune Afrique Livres

Conombo, Joseph Issoufou (1989), *M'ba Tinga: traditions des Mossé dans l'empire du Mogho-Naaba*, Paris: Harmattan

Giri, Jacques (1989), *Le Sahel au XXIe Siècle*, Paris: Karthala

Ki-Zerbo, Joseph (1978), *Histoire de l'Afrique noire*, Paris: Hatier

Martens, Ludo (1989), *Sankara, Compaoré et la révolution* burkinabè, *Brussels: Editions EPO*

'Retour au Burkina' (dossier) (1989), *Politique Africaine*, No 33

Tapsoba, Francois and Claude-Guy Pilon (1989), *Burkina Faso*, Ouagadougou: Aide à l'enfance-Canade

Tauxier, Louis (ed.) (1985), *Contes du Burkina*, Paris: Edicef

ABOUT THE AUTHOR

Robin Sharp was a broadcaster and foreign correspondent until joining Oxfam as a researcher and lobbyist in the mid-1970s. More recently he has been editor of the magazine *Development*, and the organiser of an international conference of non-governmental agencies, the World Food Assembly. He is currently a programme director at the International Institute for Environment and Development, working closely with development groups in the Sahel and other parts of Africa.

OTHER BOOKS IN OXFAM'S COUNTRY BRIEF SERIES:

Already published:

Bangladesh: The Strength To Succeed by Jim Monan
Mozambique: A Cry For Peace by Julian Quan
Namibia: Apartheid's Forgotten Children by Caroline Moorehead
Sudan: The Roots Of Famine by Nick Cater

Forthcoming:

India: An Oxfam Report by Julia Mosse
Vietnam: An Oxfam Report by Larry Jagan

For details of how to order these and other publications from Oxfam, please write to Oxfam Publications for a copy of our annual catalogue of available titles.

Oxfam Publications, Oxfam, 274 Banbury Road, Oxford OX2 7DZ

(Mark Edwards/Oxfam)